CW00454805

FINANCIAL PLANNING FOR ENTREPRENEURS

HOW TO BUILD YOUR OWN ROUTE TO FINANCIAL INDEPENDENCE

JAMES WOODFALL

R^ethink

First published in Great Britain 2020
by Rethink Press (www.rethinkpress.com)

© Copyright James Woodfall

All rights reserved. No part of this publication may be
reproduced, stored in or introduced into a retrieval system,
or transmitted, in any form, or by any means (electronic,
mechanical, photocopying, recording or otherwise) without
the prior written permission of the publisher.

The right of James Woodfall to be identified as the author of
this work has been asserted by him in accordance with the
Copyright, Designs and Patents Act 1988.

This book is sold subject to the condition that it shall not,
by way of trade or otherwise, be lent, resold, hired out, or
otherwise circulated without the publisher's prior consent
in any form of binding or cover other than that in which it
is published and without a similar condition including this
condition being imposed on the subsequent purchaser.

Disclaimer

*The views expressed in this book do not constitute financial advice.
The investment ideas discussed should never be used without first
assessing your own financial situation and consulting a qualified
financial adviser. Neither the author nor the publisher can be held
responsible for any losses that may result from investments made
after reading this book.*

Contents

Introduction

I've worked as a financial planner since 2008 and I set up my own business in 2014. Over the years I've worked with many clients in a variety of financial circumstances

The case study below tells the story of two imagined clients, Mark and Sam, who each have a different attitude to money and have chosen very different paths. Their stories bring to life some of the dilemmas facing entrepreneurs when making decisions about their financial future.

CASE STUDY: A TALE OF TWO ENTREPRENEURS

In 2050, Mark was 65 years old and by that point had been retired for seven years, after running his own business for thirty-three years. He had not had a lot of success after university, struggling to find a place on the corporate ladder. University was great, and left him with amazing friendships but unprepared for the world of work. The first job he had out of university was for a recruitment company, specialising in placing candidates in sales positions. He hated it. It never felt like it suited him; he only took the job as he was struggling to find one after the financial crash of 2008. The pay was OK and covered student loan repayments, the rent plus a few basic expenses, but the main proportion of Mark's earnings came through commissions. This was hard; it meant that from month to month Mark felt like he had no money at all and then all of a sudden several candidates would be placed and a large bonus payment would come in.

Over the lean months, he had spent money on going out, clothes, meals and sporting events. However, his credit card balance was rarely cleared in full. The rest of his bonus payments went on holidays and one-off expenses. There was never any left over for saving. The culture at the company he worked for was cut-throat and once, when Mark was on holiday, a colleague called his candidates and told them he had left the company, in order to steal his commissions. His boss did little about this and so Mark left. After a string of other unsuccessful jobs, Mark decided to start his own business. At 25 he fell back on his previous career knowledge and set up his own recruitment company.

Mark had a friend from uni, Sam. Sam had always wanted to be a pilot and after uni he applied for an airline's training academy. He had some savings that his parents had put aside for him from an early age, and he put some of that towards the cost of his training. After three years of training he became a pilot and enjoyed flying around the world, visiting many different places. Sam had always been sensible with money, and since most of his expenses were paid for when at work, he managed to save a large portion of his earnings each month. His parents had spoken to him about the importance of saving when he was young, and it's something he had always done, saving his pocket money from an early age. As a result, he avoided debt and only spent money on the things he needed.

The first few years in business for Mark were hard; finding clients was difficult and Mark found himself working all the hours he could. He would console himself by thinking 'one day it will all be easy'. With no money available in the early years to take on a team to support him, Mark found himself stretched thinly. Every evening and weekend were filled with work, and friendships eventually withered away. At 30, Mark got married and not long after had his first child. As business started to go well, he bought a house for his growing family. He still found himself working many hours and often, if they went away on holiday, Mark would have an eye on his phone or be on his laptop working. He was never really present with his family.

At 35, Sam also settled down and started a family. His job involved being away for days at a time, but then when he was at home he made sure his mind was not on work. Over time, this started to worry Sam. With a young family, he felt as though he was missing out, sometimes. His mother, Gail, worked as a financial planner and he asked her for some help. What Sam wanted to do was train as an instructor and maybe open his own flying school. There was a grass airfield near where he lived, and he thought that would be the perfect place to set up his own business. He was not sure whether he could afford to, although his earnings from work were still allowing him to save each month. When wondering whether to start the business, his concern was whether it would mean less pay, so he would no longer be saving as much for the future. Gail helped her son work out what he would need each month to meet the cost of his lifestyle, and also think ahead for what he might spend in later life. The airline Sam worked for offered a generous pension scheme and, combined with his savings, that meant he was already fairly well-off. Gail helped show Sam that he could afford to take a reduction in pay, and save a lower amount. Confident in his mother's advice, Sam quit at 40 and set up his own flying school at the airfield near his home.

Although Mark was earning a good income from the business, his expenses had increased at the same rate as income had gone up. As quickly as Mark earned it, it seemed to disappear. The money that he had been spending in his twenties on going out with friends had been replaced with a mortgage, children and running a household. There was still little left over at the end of the month. When Mark hit 55, he had an offer from someone who wanted to buy his business. The offer was a partial payment upfront, with a balance payable over three years, on condition Mark stayed in the business to help with the handover.

The payout was great and with it Mark paid off his mortgage, gave some money to each of his two children and had a family holiday. The rest of it Mark invested himself. Having worked in recruitment all these years, he decided that he had an eye for companies that were good employers. He invested in shares of companies he knew a bit about: some old clients and others he had done some limited research on. Over the next three years, the handover of the company didn't go very well and the final payment Mark was expecting didn't come through, as the business hadn't hit its turnover target. As much as Mark argued that was unfair, he had to concede as the contract he had signed gave him no option. At 58, he retired and fully left his business.

Sam ran the flying school successfully, and his enthusiasm for flying meant he had several students coming to him by recommendation. With home just around the corner, he'd spend lots of quality time with his family. The lesson he had learned while working at the airline was to appreciate the time with his wife and children. So when Sam ran the flying school, he always made sure he never took his work home. His mother had retired by this point, and he took on a new financial planner to look after his investments and help Sam plan for the future.

Between 58 and 65, Mark continued to maintain the lifestyle he had become accustomed to and eventually started to realise he was running out of money. Not all of the investments he had made performed well, and he often tried to fix mistakes by switching investments. A stock market crash occurred when he was 62, so he sold most of the shares and put the money into his bank. Overall, Mark had lost more money than he made. When friends asked him for advice, he would tell them investment was a waste of time and not to bother.

As Sam grew older, he started thinking about how he might hand over the running of the flying school to someone else. He had recruited and trained a few instructors, but one really stood out. Eventually Sam sat down with her and asked whether she wanted to take over the running of the school. Sam had continued working with his financial planner, who by this point had calculated that he had accumulated enough wealth that he no longer needed to work – he was financially independent. Knowing this, Sam decided to hand over the running of the flying school and 50% of the shares to his new business partner. The deal was that he would continue to teach whenever he liked, but no longer had to deal with all the finance and admin side of the business (the bit he had never really enjoyed).

Now 65, Mark is seriously worried about what will happen in the future. With his savings running out, he is thinking he might have to go back to work, or sell the house and buy a smaller property. Even then, he is not sure whether that will be enough. In a chance encounter, though, he got back in touch with Sam and they arranged to meet up for lunch.

Over the table the two friends swapped stories of what they had been up to over the years, reminisced about the time they spent together at university and talked about their families. They spoke about work and their experiences running businesses, and it began to occur to Mark that, while it sounded like they had shared similar struggles balancing work and family, Sam seemed to be far happier. Sam had always thought that Mark was living a great life; they were friends on social media and Sam had been used to seeing photos of Mark's holidays and new toys. Eventually, Mark confided in Sam and mentioned he had been struggling financially since he sold the business. Sam seemed surprised, as he had the impression Mark had sold for a lot of money and no longer had to work.

Mark asked Sam what his secret had been, and Sam put it down to having always saved from an early age. He spoke about his parents and the education about money they had given him. Mark said that he couldn't recall ever having a conversation about money with his mother and father. Sam mentioned that the pension he had from the airline was a great help, too. Mark had never had a pension; he had thought about setting one up but never got around to it.

Leaving the lunch, Mark was starting to realise he had not taken the right approach with money all these years. He had spent rather than saved, sacrificed time with his family for work and, to be truthful, hadn't enjoyed working in recruitment for years. He had always wanted to do something else, but was always worried that he couldn't afford to. Thinking back, he knew he should have sold the recruitment business years before he did, when he fell out of love with it. The problem wasn't that Mark didn't have any other ideas, it was that he never got around to them. He was always busy and time slipped away. The years had flown by so fast, Mark was left wondering what had happened. At 65, he is running the risk of running out of money and having to consider what few options he has.

EXERCISE

Think about the contrasting cases of Mark and Sam. Did you identify strongly with one or the other? Make a note of any parallels in your own financial circumstances that reflect those of the characters. What would you like to change about your own financial situation?

The role that money plays in our lives has always interested me. It is the currency of living. Money plays a part in incentivising entrepreneurs to do great things. There are many creative ways we can earn it, and finding ways of doing so is highly enjoyable. We can use it in many ways too: we can spend it, give it away or save it. Many uses can be found for money, to create experiences in our lives that bring joy to us and those we choose to spend our time with.

It's not all positive, of course. While money creates opportunity, it can also trap us. We can live our lives in fear of never having enough, or of running out. That can mean we hang onto money when we don't need to, or risk living a miserable life in poverty. Not knowing how much money you need in your life means a life of uncertainty. The decisions you make about your career, business and the lifestyle you have will be limited by an uncertain future. What if you knew exactly how much money you needed in your life, and knew exactly how to go about accumulating it?

Financial independence is particularly important for business owners. Entrepreneurs setting up their own businesses should understand the financial risks and rewards involved in their own enterprise. However, the pressure to maintain and grow a new business, and to take care of its financial health, means it can be easy to overlook your own personal financial security in the long term. How can you ensure your own position in later life resembles Sam's comfortable security, rather than Mark's precarious retirement?

That is what this book is about. My aim is to get you thinking about the role that money plays in your life in new ways, and give you practical tools that help you plan for the future. There is no get-rich-quick solution contained in here; this is about a healthy, life-long relationship with money that allows you to make better decisions and improve your happiness.

At relevant points throughout the book you will find a link to the Financial Health Check Scorecard (https://woodfallwealth.scoreapp.com). This score-card has been devised to analyse five core categories of your financial health – budgeting, borrowing, taxation, planning for the future and protecting yourself from risks. It asks a series of thought-provoking questions to get you thinking about your attitude to money and your financial habits, presenting a snap-shot of where you are and some potential areas for your financial growth. You may find it helpful to use the scorecard alongside this book.

In the book, I will start by helping you understand your purpose and the role that money plays. Then I will explain some tools and concepts to get you think-ing about planning for the future. Finally, I will look at what to consider when you reach that future. I hope you enjoy reading it as much as I have enjoyed writing it.

1

How To Define Purpose

During the Covid-19 pandemic in 2020, many people got a sense of what their eventual retirement might feel like. In the UK, a large number of workers were furloughed and stayed at home, on 80% pay but with no work to do. As a consequence, they were gaining an insight into the experience of retirees: the sudden loss of work pushed people into finding projects to fill their time and give them a sense of purpose. But once you have cleaned the car, baked bread, spring-cleaned the house and completed do-it-yourself (DIY) projects – what next?

I read *How to Create a Mind* by Ray Kurzweil recently, and I was interested to see the subject of purpose come up. The people investing their time and effort into building artificial intelligence (AI) have had to understand how elements of the human brain work. Take purpose for an example: to build an AI, you have to define what purpose is before you can give it to the AI. The definition of purpose in *How to Create a Mind* is simply this: a series of small goals.

When we set goals for ourselves, there is a tendency to tell ourselves 'I'll be happy when I've achieved x or y'. The problem is, when we get the thing we were aiming for, we are no longer happy. The reason is that we no longer have anything to aim for and so feel a sense of purposelessness. Not long after you get what you wanted, you decide you want something else.

What makes us content is not the achievement of our goals, it's the process of setting goals and the journey towards achievement. The end result can provide short-term gratification, but ultimately leave us unfulfilled.

Life in lockdown gave people insight into what it feels like to have your sense of purpose taken away. For most of us, our main goals tend to focus around our work and career. Not everyone can work from home, so take that away and it leaves us in a state of limbo. Out of work, our hobbies and interests provide us with another opportunity for a sense of purpose through progression, but during the lockdowns of 2020 many could not even pursue their hobbies.

In *Life 3.0* by Max Tegmark there is an interesting thought about how to give people purpose without jobs. One of the factors that boosts people's sense of wellbeing and purpose is the sense of pleasure one gets from doing something one is good at and operating within a state of flow, a concept first articulated by Mihaly Csikszentmihalyi in *Flow: the psychology of optimal experience.* Learning from this, a lifetime goal to help you gain fulfilment is to always be engaging in a series of small projects, using your skill set in a flow state.

When you operate in a state of flow you feel present and deeply distracted by the task at hand. You don't have time to worry about the past or feel anxious about the future. Your mind is elsewhere, focusing on the job in front of you. This flow state can be relaxing for some. I find that I get the greatest sense of this when I am doing something manual. I fell in love with sailing a few years ago and, for me, it's the best way to switch off into a state of flow and relaxation.

In my experience, when I ask people what they are going to do when they retire, the answer often is 'I don't know'. I often find the real answer is 'I haven't thought about it'.

The aim of retirement shouldn't be to finally finish work with nothing to do. When you arrive at that point, without continuing to set a series of goals, unhappiness and boredom will creep in. This came up not that long ago in conversation with a friend of mine, who said their newly retired parents had bought a camper van and set themselves the goal of camping at the highest point in each county in the UK. That will take some time and is a great way to bring a sense of purpose to life. It is measurable, too, and progress can be tracked as each county is ticked off the list.

Goals keep us engaged with life and to lose them means losing a sense of purpose. Through all stages of life, create small goals for things you enjoy doing, not just for your career. One way of ensuring that you maintain a sense of purpose later in life is this – don't retire!

What gives you fulfilment and meaning?

Working on this concept of a series of small goals, what do you do in your life that gives you the most fulfilment and meaning?

EXERCISE

Think of a time when you were operating in a complete state of flow, completely absorbed in what you were doing and content. What were you doing?

What was it about that activity that you found fulfilling?

Think now, what are the three things you could do right away to create more time to do that?

You may have found that what you wrote down wasn't related to your business and work; or that, if it was, it may have only been a part of what you do in your business. The idea that the best business is that which allows you to make a living from doing the thing you love is a myth. The initial idea may be something that you are passionate about, but the nature of most small businesses is that most of the work the owner ends up doing isn't the part they love. In the Introduction we read about Mark starting his business and having to do every single job in the company. Now, some of those jobs are not going to be ones you enjoy all that much, or are even that skilled at.

Over time something which you find fulfilling is at risk of becoming mundane if you do it day in, day out with no change or growth. Take your favourite film: if you watched it two or three times in a row that might be OK, but ten? You would soon get bored of watching the same scenes over and over again.

This means that, to keep doing work that you find fulfilling and meaningful, you need to constantly be looking at new ideas and ways that you can grow and develop. You need to create a series of small goals and enjoy the journey along the path to growth.

In completing the exercise, you may have come up with something that was completely unrelated to your work. That does not mean that you need to change your work; what it means is that you need to view your company as a tool for creating more time to allow you to do the things that give the most fulfilment and meaning to your life.

I love sailing. A few years ago, when my wife and I became engaged, we decided that our ideal honeymoon would be a couple of weeks sailing around the Caribbean. In our mind we had the image of the two of us sailing a yacht on our own around islands, stopping off at a different location each night. The only problem was, neither of us knew how to sail. For the next six months, I went on training courses to learn the practice and theory of sailing, and I became a qualified skipper by the end of them. Our honeymoon was perfect and we had two weeks with just the two of us sailing around the British Virgin Islands.

When we came back, we realised that we were strongly attracted to the peace and quiet that sailing provides you. We found that when we are away on a yacht, our focus is completely on what we are doing at the present moment and we don't have time to think about work. We completely switch off from our normal lives and, when we return home, we are refreshed and recharged. Our aim now is to create more time to go on sailing adventures.

Life is suffering

The Dalai Lama is widely reported, when asked about what surprised him most about humanity, to have answered:

'Man. Because he sacrifices his health in order to make money. Then he sacrifices money to recuperate his health. And then he is so anxious about the future that he does not enjoy the present; the result being that he does not live in the present or the future; he lives as if he is never going to die; and then dies having never really lived.'[1]

Life is stressful and that is something you come to terms with and accept. Along your journey there will be bumps in the road and at times you may feel that you don't see the point in what you are doing. I've learned that this never goes away and needs to be managed throughout life.

One cause of this feeling is that we get most satisfaction from the journey towards attaining a goal, not the attainment itself. When we achieve things that we are aiming for, when we get there, we feel unfulfilled as there is no longer anything to aim for. So we start to look at what the next thing is, and the thing after that. The goal we just attained diminishes in gratifying us. If you were aiming to buy the car of your dreams, let's say a Ferrari, once you had done so you would be happy and feel a rush of the pleasure hormone dopamine. But once that wore off, you would probably start looking for a car that is better than yours

---

1   The quote cannot be reliably attributed to the Dalai Lama; however, I have chosen to include it as its author has perfectly summarised a modern dilemma.

and then want that. When this process starts, the car you once dreamed of and worked hard to get now no longer gives you the same pleasure. The attainment of our goals keeps us happy for a short time, whereas the journey to attainment keeps us engaged and motivated far longer.

This is part of the nature of life as suffering. There are always things that you don't enjoy doing, and stresses in life, but most of us accept that it is part of the journey. As business owners, this is evident and shows up all over the place.

When we set long-term goals for ourselves, we run the risk of losing our connection with the present. Long-term goals are a great way of stretching yourself, giving direction and motivation. However, when we set a goal for ourselves either we are going to achieve it, or we are not. What happens is we create in our minds a future version of ourselves and then worry about it, creating anxiety in the present moment. There is a balance between setting goals for direction and growth, and becoming so obsessed with the achievement of those goals that we lose sight of the present moment.

Plans can change and obstacles can get in the way of us achieving the things we set out to. As we've already discussed, the journey is more fulfilling than the arrival. So set big, ambitious goals, and keep your attention on enjoying the present moment.

Life is not a rehearsal

Memento mori – remember that you, too, must die.

Death can be a taboo subject in the UK and we don't like to talk about it. The fact is, it happens to all of us and we usually have no idea when. None of us know what mysteries lurk on the other side of death, and perhaps that is one reason to fear it. There is one thing we can be certain of, we don't get another go at the life we are living right now. Why are we discussing death in a book about money? Put simply, because time is slipping away from you and death approaching far quicker than you realise. Because we don't talk about death, at first it never really occurs to us that one day we are going to die. As we get older it occurs to us more often, as we see each year go by quicker and quicker.

When you were 5 years old, how much time passed between each Christmas? It felt like ages and now once one is over the next one appears, before you have even finished thinking about the last. Of course, this is relative; when you were 5 years old a year represented 20% of your life. As you get older, naturally a year becomes a shorter and shorter proportion of the time you have experienced in your life.

This means that the older you get, the quicker time seems to pass, and it seems to get faster and faster. Before you realise, you are at the end of your life, looking back and wondering 'what happened and where did all that time go?' Ask the older generations in your family what they think of this; they will tell you it's all too true.

Marcus Aurelius was a Roman Emperor from 161 to 180 CE, and studied Stoic philosophy. During his reign, his philosophical views governed the way he acted. He kept a personal book of his own thoughts, which was eventually published after his death. The *Meditations* of Marcus Aurelius contain some important wisdom on life and specifically this phenomenon of life being short. If you think about your whole lifetime, there is a period at the beginning where we are children and reliant upon our parents for care. We are restricted in what we can do in these years due to our youth. The same occurs at the end of our life, although we may not think that way. At the end of your life there are potentially a number of years where your health will hold you back. You will not be able to live life as fully as in your younger years. This means we are left with the bit in the middle, making life far shorter than we realise.

Marcus Aurelius muses quite often about time in the *Meditations*, at one point comparing the end-of-life period to being trapped in a corpse. A slightly harsh way of putting it! Consider the amount of time that the universe has been around: 13.8 billion years. The useful part of a human life is insignificant in comparison. Thinking about your own mortality is a great way to put into perspective what is important. With the time you have left, do you really want to waste time on trivial matters that will soon be forgotten?

Try this now: think of something that is really bothering you right now. Could be work, could be personal; it doesn't matter which, for this exercise. Now imagine the end of your life and become fully aware of the fact that one day you are going to die. This is non-negotiable and none of us have any control over when it might happen. As you focus on your mortality, you start to realise that what little time you have left is not meant to be spent worrying about trivial things. Now, things happen in life that do persist, that don't disappear overnight and that do take longer to deal with. These can still be considered within the context of your own mortality and the time you have left. A key part of stoicism is the belief that, although we cannot change what has happened, we can change how we think about it.

We need reminding that time is slipping away from us and, if you are around middle age and thinking the first half has gone quickly, the second half will be faster still. The reason we need reminding about this reality is that we get distracted by our busy lives.

Busy being busy

Have you ever had a day in which you were really busy? Where you jumped from one thing to the next and felt rushed off your feet all day? Doesn't time feel as though it passes even quicker on days like those? Now, what about a day where you sat around with nothing to do; didn't time feel as though it was passing far more slowly?

When we are busy, with work or our lives outside work, time passes faster than we realise. We focus on the short term, on what we are doing right now and what is coming up next. Long-term thinking is something that you get round to when you put time aside and, if you are like most people, you also put off planning for the things you always want to do – those bucket list items, that holiday home, or that second business or career. The problem is, as time passes especially quickly when we are busy, we get to the end of our lives before we realise and look back with regret.

The problem with being busy all the time and time flying by, is that we struggle to make time for the important things in life. Even when we try to switch off, we have busy minds. Have you ever had a holiday where you thought it took at least three days before you stopped thinking about work? It happens to me all the time. Although I stop checking my emails or answering the phone on holiday, I still can't switch my brain off straight away. What this means is that you can be standing watching a gorgeous sunset on a Greek island, and just as the sun dips below the horizon and you wonder whether you will see the mythical 'green flash', your mind wanders into thinking about what you have to do when you get back to the office.

It's too easy to work all hours available at the moment. Having work emails on your phone means there is a sneaky, back-door way for companies to stay in touch with you all the time. Even if you are on holiday, they may expect you to check your emails, or reply to something important. I'd argue that their definition of importance is open to interpretation. If you have a job that comes with a mobile and a laptop, so you can 'work from home', this means that you will be working from home. There is always a temptation to do a few hours that evening or reply to your emails on a Sunday before you get to the office on Monday. All of this leads to one thing – you never switch off. Before mobile phones and laptops, if you needed to work late then you had to stay in the office. Today, it's more subtle and we can easily slip into working at home.

The problem with work creeping into the home is that it can interfere with the attention we give our partners and families. We can be too tired from work to even think about money and planning. Things get put off, and if put off for too long this starts having negative effects.

Ikigai – your reason to get up in the morning

In Japanese, there is a word that means 'your reason to jump out of bed each morning', or 'your reason for being'. It is *ikigai* (pronounced ee-kee-guy).

In their book, *Ikigai: The Japanese Secret to a Long and Happy Life,* Hector Garcia and Francesc Miralles illustrate ten ways of living a great life:

1. Stay active and don't retire

2. Leave urgency behind and adopt a slower pace of life

3. Only eat until you are 80% full

4. Surround yourself with good friends

5. Get in shape through daily, gentle exercise

6. Smile and acknowledge people around you

7. Reconnect with nature

8. Give thanks to anything that brightens your day and makes you feel alive

9. Live in the moment

10. Follow your *ikigai.*

Staying active and not retiring are highly important for our long-term happiness. The concept of retiring scares a lot of people, in my experience: the thought of getting to a future date where, all of a sudden, the career you have built for the 40+ years preceding, disappears overnight. Successful retirement is knowing who you are and what you get fulfilment from. The idea shouldn't be to get to a date in the future and suddenly fall off a cliff; it should be to find purpose and meaning by continuing to do the things that you find fulfilling. The change may be that you no longer get all this fulfilment from your work; you need to come up with ideas and ways of achieving this outside your work (or rather, your business).

Ikigai can be seen as the point where four crucial elements of your business overlap:

Ikigai (diagram adapted from M Winn, 'What is your Ikigai?')

Dan Buettner, interviewed by Cathy Newman in *National Geographic*,[2] highlights the concept of *ikigai* as one of the reasons for the health and long life of

---

2   Cathy Newman, 'How to live to a ripe old age', *National Geographic*, 29 December 2012.

the Okinawans. In Okinawa, many people continue to perform their jobs for as long as they remain healthy. The idea of retiring doesn't seem to appeal as much to them, and it's far more common that people keep working.

In their paper 'Mental retirement', written in 2010, Susann Rohwedder and Robert J. Willis investigated the effects of early retirement on cognition through surveying older persons across the US, the UK and eleven EU countries. Their conclusion was that 'early retirement has a significant negative impact on the cognitive ability of people in their early 60s'.

Continuing to undertake work we find gives us purpose and meaning isn't just good for our happiness, it is crucial for our health.

Life planning

Now I want to make something clear here: I don't believe in planning your life to such a level of detail that it becomes binary. A great part of life is making unexpected discoveries. However, some of the greatest discoveries come from doing things that have been planned. Have you ever travelled to a different country and returned with a new perspective on your life? You might have planned the trip, but couldn't have planned how you felt about the experience.

Part of the process of planning your life is identifying specific activities you want to do and, most importantly, stating clearly when you are going to do them. Instead of thinking 'I've always wanted to go to... ', make a plan and book the trip. It's far easier to get on a plane if you have a ticket.

Not something you find, it's something you have to create

The opportunity to create income and wealth comes at the cost of sacrificing hours and hours of your time. The risk is that what was once exciting and new slips into being mundane and boring and time can pass far more quickly than we realise in this state.

When we create goals for growth, it is the process of setting goals and then working towards attainment that gives us the most fulfilment in our lives. However, to get closer to living a great life you need to enjoy the journey in the present and not be distracted too much by the attainment of your goals. Forsaking the present for the future is a formula for unhappiness. We create a future in our minds and then become so attached to it that we worry about whether or not it will happen. In doing so, we forget to enjoy the present.

To live a life of fulfilment, think about who you are and what is important to you. What is it that you do that gives you the most purpose and meaning to your life? If it is within your business, one thing to aim for is to set up your business so that it allows you to focus on the activities that you find most rewarding. Outside the business and work, create more time to spend doing things you enjoy with people that you love.

2

How Do You Think About Money?

Financial Literacy

When you think about your relationship with money, what comes to mind? Our money habits are learned from an early age, and yet financial education is not a major curriculum subject. When teachers in the UK were surveyed in 2017 by Young Money,[3] 94% agreed or strongly agreed that financial education gives students an essential life skill, and 95% of teachers feel it is important.

Having financial literacy is key to being able to understand the value of money and how to manage it. If the

---

3   For more on financial education of young people, see www.young-enterprise.org.uk/home/impact-policy/research-evaluation/research/impact-of-financial-education

basic knowledge isn't there, it can be hard to hold onto money when you make it. Concepts like saving regularly, using debt wisely and managing risks effectively might seem common sense to some, yet when Yorkshire Building Society undertook a poll of 2,000 people in 2019, they found that nearly one in six had no savings at all. Also, 26% could not last for a whole month on their savings. The initial assumption that could be drawn is that this only applies to low earners – but that isn't the case. Of those earning over £100,000 per annum, 40% did not have more than three months' expenses saved, compared to 48% of lower-income participants in the survey.[4]

So what is going on? We live in a world of ever-increasing instant gratification. If you want something, you can buy it online, and in some cities have it delivered the same day, if not the next day. If you don't have the money, not a problem: you can buy now and pay later or use credit cards. The latest credit trend I've seen is 'buy now pay later' credit providers teaming up with retailers, including clothing retailers. What was once unaffordable suddenly becomes affordable if you spread the cost in monthly instalments.

The issue with this is that something like fashion and clothing is for some a monthly purchase. By accumulating debt under 'buy now pay later' schemes you are

---

4   Yorkshire Building Society, 'Exploring the UK's Attitude to Saving Money', 2019.

kicking the can down the road, creating a far bigger problem later on.

University of Cambridge behaviour experts David Whitebread and Sue Bingham carried out research in 2013 and found that our money habits are formed by age 7.[5] The way we plan ahead and deal with delaying gratification is set by the time we reach 7 years of age. Once those habits are formed, it can be hard to change them later in life.

It's never too late to learn good money habits, but research suggests that a better way of ensuring that your children have a good start is to teach them about money habits from an early age.

Take a minute to think about your current money habits.

EXERCISE

How do you deal with delaying gratification?

How do you plan for the future?

Do you budget?

If you have debt, is it being used wisely?

Do you save and invest regularly?

---

5   David Whitebread and Sue Bingham, 'Habit Formation and Learning in Young Children', Money Advice Service, 2013.

> To undertake a more detailed analysis of your financial health, try completing the Financial Health Check Scorecard at https://woodfallwealth.scoreapp.com.

Money is a tool to get you great experiences

Experiences are more important than stuff. I've talked already about the short-term gratification that comes from owning things. The problem is, that once you have the thing in your possession, after time you move on to the next thing. And so that repeats.

Research has suggested that people are waking up to this and leading the way are millennials, who are valuing experiences over material possessions. It's not just millennials, though; people of all ages value experiences over things. A study conducted by Expedia and the Center for Generational Kinetics found that 74% of people asked in the USA value experiences over things. The same study found that the experience that is most valued among all ages and income brackets is travel.[6]

The feeling we get from buying things is nothing more than a chemical reaction. The chemical is called dopamine and it is a hormone that the brain produces when we accomplish a task, exercise or get a promotion, for example. It is our chemical reward for

6   Expedia and the Center for Generational Kinetics, 'Generations on the Move', 2018.

achieving something and plays a role in our motivation. It is also released in anticipation when we buy things we want. When we purchase something that we have desired, we get a hit of dopamine making us feel great, but once this wears off we no longer feel so great and buyer's regret kicks in. This reward mechanism is how gamblers become addicted and the same can happen for shoppers.

We live in a world of instant gratification, where we can buy most things that we desire on the same day. When I was sitting in lockdown owing to the coronavirus, I ordered a book I wanted to read. The delivery stated it was going to take a whole week to come. As irrational as it sounds, I noticed a small part of me becoming impatient at having to wait a week. This is the impact that instant gratification has had on us and it is hard to escape if you have become used to it.

Payment company Klarna has boomed in recent years and offers people shopping with partner retailers the opportunity to buy things before they get paid. This does not encourage good money habits, and only satisfies the need for instant gratification. Schemes like Klarna offer purchasers the items they want, before they know they can pay for these items, and deferred payment. For clothing retailers especially, this means that their customers can make larger orders online than they can afford, knowing they can send back what they don't want to keep before the payment is due. Retailers have embraced this because the overall spend under this scheme increases. Customers end up spending far more than they would if they had to pay for the items at the point of sale.

We get more satisfaction out of spending time with people we love, doing things that fascinate us, than we do from shopping. One pleasure is short, the other provides a lifetime of memories and experiences that broaden our horizons.

The aim of managing money for happiness is to ensure that you get the most reward from what you spend your money on, and to do that you have to practise delaying gratification, be aware of any desires to seek gratification and manage your own emotions. A few ways that you can manage a need for gratification are:

- *Think:* is this something that I need right now or is something that I want?

- *Wait* a week before making a large purchase; if you have a partner, discuss it with them – they may have a different perspective to you and be able to make an impartial decision about whether it is something you need or want.

- *Have a bigger goal to refer to*, like financial independence, so you can make a comparison and decide whether the short-term spend will delay you getting something you want more.

A good way to measure success?

Money is used by many as a barometer for how successful a person is. The more money they have, the greater success they appear to have achieved. The outside signs of a person with money don't tell you how it was earned, or whether it was inherited or won in a lottery. Sometimes a person who has the outward signs of wealth may be showing off items that have been obtained on credit. You can buy a Rolex on credit, your car on hire purchase, your holiday in instalments. You can easily fool people into perceiving you as wealthy. However, a lifestyle maintained through credit isn't sustainable for long.

One of the many problems with social media is distinguishing between how much of what we see is real and how much is fake. Humans are social animals and we are heavily influenced by what others do. The term for it is social proof, and it influences us in a number of ways, from what we buy to whether we help someone in need. Related to this is the bystander effect: when someone is in distress and needs help, a crowd of people will look at what each other is doing before they act. They will wait to see whether someone else will be first to offer help. Once one person helps, others may follow, but the initial aid can be delayed while people are paralysed, waiting to see who goes first. It's safer to have a heart attack in a quiet road with one or two other people around, than in a crowded place.

FINANCIAL PLANNING FOR ENTREPRENEURS

We are influenced by what we see others do and, accordingly, money may not be the best measure of success. Several lottery winners have come into vast amounts of money, amounts that would be life-changing for many, only to spend them frivolously and in a few years end up with nothing to show for it. One lottery winner who ended with nothing in the space of ten years stated that going broke was the best thing to happen to him and that he would advise anyone against quitting work.[7]

In over fourteen years of talking to people about their money, I have come to the conclusion that there is no relationship between the amount of money someone has and their happiness. If I consider my own situation for a moment and compare where I am now to where I was fifteen years ago, my income and assets are far higher, but I wouldn't say that the same multiple applies to how happy I am. We worry about not having enough money, but once that worry goes away our happiness doesn't increase drastically. Once you have a basic amount of money available to live life on your own terms, more isn't necessarily going to increase your wellbeing.

The term 'keeping up with the Joneses' originates either from Mark Twain or from a comic strip by Arthur R. Momand from 1913. In the UK, you might remember the TV programme *Keeping up Appearances*,

---

7   Gary O'Shea and Alison Maloney, 'No regrets', *The Sun*, 11 February 2019.

which ran from 1990 to 1995. The programme made fun of the social class structure in the UK, with the character Hyacinth Bucket insisting her surname is pronounced 'Bouquet'. Social pressure can affect our spending habits, and the stereotypical 'keeping up with the Joneses' scenario would be: neighbour A gets new windows, neighbour B copies them; then neighbour A gets a new driveway and so does B; A gets a hot tub for the garden, B follows. Today, the Joneses are not just the people living either side of us; we are friends with them on social media. If your social status is defined by what you possess, then social media can greatly influence how you use your money.

How much money do you need for the rest of your life?

So, how do you answer the question 'how much money do I need to live comfortably?'

Before you can work out what you need for the rest of your life, you need to define what living a great life on your own terms looks like. This requires looking at what your lifestyle costs today and what it might cost in the future.

If you have a pension in the UK, you will usually receive a statement each year telling you how much income it is projected to provide at retirement. This is based on assumptions about inflation, investment growth rates and how long you will live, that are based on Office for National Statistics data. It is assumed that you will require the same income for the entirety of your retirement – but this is false. Our costs tend to reduce the older we get and, after a certain age, for health reasons we may be unable to do the things we could when we were younger. While our ability to live lives as full as those of our earlier years may affect how much we spend, care costs become a reality for many. The cost of care in later life can mean a sudden spike in spending in those last years. Life is short as we have established, but when you take into account that there is a period towards the end of life where you can't do the things you used to be able to, life becomes even shorter.

With this in mind, to work out how much money we need to live life on our terms, we need to think about the current cost of our lifestyle, what our lifestyle might cost in the future when we reduce or stop working, and then assume that our leisure costs decrease towards the end of our life. Then we can start to think about how much money is required to pay for all of that, and for costs we don't like to think about, such as health, care and funerals. Some of course will be paid for by income from the work we choose to do, but some will need to be saved for. We also need to factor in that we can't put off the things we want to do for too long, as we have no control over when our lives might change, or have to change. However, time speeds up the older we get and it will come around quicker than we realise.

You also need to think about when you plan to reduce working or stop working and start doing the things that give you purpose and meaning. These may or may not mean an increase in your lifestyle costs. Once this has been established, the amount of money you need to save can be calculated. We will discuss in Chapter 6 how to do that, but for now we are introducing the concept of financial independence.

Financial independence is having enough accumulated in assets that you can live off the income and capital for the rest of your life. From then on, you work because you choose to, not because you have to. There is a difference and when it comes to having the freedom to do work that gives purpose and meaning to your life, being financially independent is an important milestone.

Why knowing your number is essential to any financial plan

The 100-year life is more common now than ever before. Data from the Office for National Statistics shows that a 30-year old man has a 7.4% chance of living to 100, and a 30-year old woman has a 10.9% chance.[8]

---

8   Office for National Statistics, 'Life Expectancy Calculator', 2019.

The average retirement age in the UK is 65, which means that those who live to 100 will spend thirty-five years in retirement. If we assume that the average age of starting work after education is 22, then that means forty-three years spent working, only eight more years than are spent in retirement.

Starting salaries in the UK probably mean that in early working life most expenditure goes on housing or living expenses, with little left for saving. It is not until salaries start rising through career progression that the majority of people have surplus income that can be saved. That may not be until your late 20s or early 30s, in my experience. This means that if saving isn't started until the age of 30, the pot that is built up between 30 and 65 has to pay not only for day-to-day living expenses, but also for future living costs. When working out how much money you need for the rest of your life, a sensible assumption is that you will live to 100. The amount of money you need for the rest of your life is a different figure for each person, but for each person it has a similar impact.

Imagine for a second that you knew now that you had enough money for the rest of your life; what work would you be doing? Would you be working? How would you spend your time? Who would you be spending your time with? What risks would you take?

The answers to these questions may give you an insight into why financial independence is an important goal. The freedom to know that you have enough money to live the rest of your life without worrying about money is all that is needed for some. However, once you have achieved financial independence, you then have complete control over how you spend your time, what you spend your time doing and who you do it with.

Many of us work because we have to, and some of us even love what we do for a living. But how many would keep working in their current role if they no longer had to? Work helps us have a sense of purpose throughout life, but financial independence allows us the freedom to engage in work that we truly find purposeful. This is different to finding purpose in the work we currently do.

Having control over your own time is a by-product of financial independence. Outside work, how many things do you do in a day that could be delegated to someone else? Freeing you up to spend more time on the activities you enjoy and that interest you. When you have control over your time, you also have control over who you spend it with. I like the quote, 'The greatest gift you can give someone is your time'. Each of us have a finite amount of it; you can withdraw but you can't deposit at the bank of time. How you spend it and who you spend it with is precious.

So, knowing how much money you need for the rest of your life gives you the freedom to spend your time as you would like, with people you love, doing things that bring purpose to your world. This is as close to a formula for a lifetime of happiness as I have been able to find.

Why financial independence should be every entrepreneur's goal

If you run a business, the dream is usually to build it up and sell it in the future, at which point you can retire comfortably on the proceeds. The problem potentially arises, come retirement time, that the owner has not thought ahead about how much money they will need to sell for. You may assume that, in the future, you will be able to sell your business: but this isn't always the case, and in Chapter 9 I will explain how you should prepare for exit.

I've met many business owners that have this dream of selling in the future and can sometimes be blinded by it – blinded to the risk that the business may fail and also blinded to the risk that they may find no one who wants to pay for it.

A business owner who is financially independent no longer relies upon selling it in the future. This means that you may feel more comfortable taking risks to grow the company, rather than playing it safe. You may find this focuses your attention on the work you love doing, and since you are financially independent, you can hire someone to do the work you don't love doing.

3
Starting To Plan

Looking back

'Twenty years from now you will be more
disappointed by the things that you didn't do
than the things that you did. So throw off the
bowlines. Sail away from the safe harbour. Catch
the trade winds in your sails. Explore. Dream.
Discover.'
 — Sarah Frances Brown[9]

This quote beautifully captures the need to seize
the day and reminds us to live life to the full, or risk
regrets later in life. However, while you may long to

---

9   In H. Jackson Brown, Jr, *P.S. I Love You* (Nashville, TN: Thomas
    Nelson, Inc., 2000 [1990]).

'sail away from the safe harbour' it can be easier said than done. If you struggle making plans for the future, putting yourself in the future and looking back can help the ideas flow.

EXERCISE

For this exercise you will need a wall, a pack of sticky notes and a note pad to write some thoughts down.

On the first note, write 0, your age when you were born and place that on the left-hand side of your wall. Take the second note, write 100, the year we assume you will live to, and place that on the far-right-hand side of the wall. Third, take a note, write your age now and place that appropriately on the timeline where you think that goes.

Now take a couple of steps back and look at your life from start to finish. What we are going to do now is start to fill in the rest of the space, starting with the events that led you to where you are today. So, beginning at the far left, start adding notes to your timeline for the key moments that made you into the person you are today. What are the events that truly shaped who you are? What are the moments that defined your beliefs and values? Fill out as many as you can and then, when you are done, take a couple of steps back again.

Looking at the moments and milestones you have just recorded, what key themes are emerging? What can you see that connects these events? If you can, summarise what links the events together in as few words as you can. If you can get it down to one word per theme, that is great. What would you say your purpose in life has been so far? What has been your reason to jump out of bed in the morning? Write your answers down as you go.

Now, let's analyse your timeline in some more detail.

Once you have done this exercise, there should be a gap with no events currently recorded – between your current age and 100. At the beginning of life, there is a childhood/youth phase lasting about twenty years, many of which we may spend in education. Later in life there is a similar period, when our mobility and health declines and we cannot live life as fully as in our younger years. Therefore, it is crucial that we plan to do the things we want to in the time that we are able to.

Starting at age 100 and working backwards, the first note to make is the age at which you think that your later life years will start. You will be left with a middle period, between your current age and the age at which you start to wind down. Remember, these middle years will go by more and more quickly as they pass. The second half will race by faster than the first, making it crucial you plan to spend time doing things you love.

Thinking back to what you wrote down about your purpose up until now, what do you want it to be in the years ahead? What specific things do you want to do in the years left? Write them down on notes and add them to the timeline. Keep filling it up until you think it is complete. To paraphrase Sarah Frances Brown, you will regret the things you didn't do, not the things you did.

One of the events might be the day you stop working, if you haven't already. To put in perspective how close you are, instead of looking at the middle period in years, think in pay days. If you are 40 and plan to retire at 65, that is 300 pay days; by the time you are 50, only 180 pay days will be left. If you have elderly members of your family, the same perspective can be applied to the time you spend with them. Let's say you have a relative who is 80, and that they are expected to live to 88. Each year you see them three times – life is hectic and you fit in a visit where you can. Looking at it another way, you have twenty-four visits left. If you knew this, what would you do differently? Would you visit more often? For longer? Do exciting things to create great memories?

In his book *Modern Man in Search of a Soul*, Carl Jung draws a parallel between the stages of life and the rising and setting of the sun. The period of youth extends up until 35–40, where the second half begins. Between the ages of 40 and 50 a change in the psyche takes place, and beliefs and values that may have been more flexible in the first half become more rigid. In this way, the second half of life is based on the principles of the first. During the first half of life, our beliefs and values are forming and being tested. We strive for security, in who we are, the partners we choose, our careers and our families. As the sun rises, it sees the light spread, and reaching greater heights spreads it wider. In youth we are optimistic and pursue growth and higher levels of success and achievement. As the sun passes noon, it declines from its peak and attention turns to its eventual setting. In the afternoon and evening, light diminishes more and more.

Jung argues that we are largely unprepared for this transition. The second half is lived in the light of the first and, while the first half light radiates outwards, in the second half light is drawn back in. The first half is dedicated to development of the individual and the second half can end up being lived in the shadow of the first, always looking back at what used to be. The solution he proposes is to ensure that the second half has a purpose of its own. When Jung wrote this in the 1930s average life expectancy was lower than it is today – the mid-point of life has been increasing steadily. If we consider the 100-year life, the mid-point is not far before the normal retirement age of 65.

Plans change; be flexible

In *Atomic Habits*, James Clear makes a good point about goal setting. When we set goals, we create two potential paths: a path to success and a path to failure. This was touched upon in 'Life planning' in chapter 1.

When you look at how you have got to where you are today, it is not that likely that you had each step mapped out and knew what you wanted twenty years before it happened, unless you decided at the age of 8 you wanted to be a doctor and have just completed your training. Most people are good at setting short-term goals – for the next three to five years, say – but even then they can change.

As we grow older, what was once important to us becomes less important. Goals we once had get replaced with ones that reflect who we are now. It is fun to revisit old goals once in a while; they might surprise you. I did this a while ago while clearing a desk out and found a book with some notes and plans I had written ten years before. It was interesting to see how many of the goals I had written down and forgotten about I had achieved. While I have different roles, responsibilities and priorities now, it made me smile that I could tick off nearly everything on the list I had made.

When setting goals, keep short- and medium-term goals specific and longer-term goals flexible. Longer-term goals can be thought of more as principles or values, things you want to have lived by or that are a theme for your life. Again, these can change, but probably not by much if you have thought about them. A lifetime goal of mine is to have made the most of opportunities to learn and grow. This principled approach allows for flexibility in my short- and medium-term goals. I can also orient what I do in the short and medium term and check whether that meets the longer-term principle.

Short- and medium-term goals are stepping stones to achieving bigger goals in the future. When you set short- and medium-term goals, put them into perspective and ask whether they take you closer to what you want in the long term.

In an appendix at the end of the book, you will find a financial plan template. This may help you to start your own planning process and begin setting your short, medium and long-term financial goals.

4

Spend Less Than You Earn

The starting point for any financial plan is making sure that the income you have coming in is more than you spend. In a 2020 survey by debt.com, of over 1,000 respondents in America, on average 80% had a household budget in place.[10] However, broken down by age group the figures show some variation across the lifespan:

Age group	Percentage who use a household budget
24 and under	76%
25–34 years old	81%
35–44 years old	79%
45–54 years old	76%
55–64 years old	79%
65 and over	82%

10   www.debt.com/research/best-way-to-budget-2019

One of the largest groups budgeting are aged 25–34, most of whom would be classed as millennials or bordering on Gen X. Millennials have been described as the generation that grew up with new technologies and is more likely to use them, which may account for the higher figures. Several banks and FinTech firms offer smart bank accounts and budgeting apps that allow to you track your spending in real time. However, millennials are also the generation that suffered the most from the 2007/08 banking crisis, with low salaries and pay rises, high housing costs and near-impossibility of being able to purchase residential property in major cities. In the early part of your career, when your earnings are at a starter level, there is a need to keep a budget to ensure that you do not overspend each month. Budgeting among this age group can be a necessity to make sure you get through the month.

For those that can't make it through the month on what is coming in, then there is a lot of temptation to use unsecured credit to fill the gap, which comes with issues I'll discuss later.

With the older generations, peak earnings for those with university degrees commonly hit in the 40s and 50s, depending on career and sector. Once you are in the position where your income comfortably exceeds your normal monthly spend, budgeting becomes less of a priority. If you know that you have a comfortable surplus each month, why go to the effort of keeping an eye on your household costs?

The problem in this scenario is that disposable income ends up being wasted on non-essentials: things end up being bought for gratification, rather than adding real value to our lives. The reason this can be problematic for some is that it can prevent you from achieving financial independence, the foundation for living a great life.

When you know how much you need to have saved to achieve financial independence, and you know how much needs to be put aside each month to accumulate that figure, then you can comfortably spend on discretionary items each month. Until you know how much of your disposable income should be saved, then be wary of how much you might be wasting each month. A sensible plan would be to keep a budget of your expenditure throughout your lifetime. If you are not aware of what your costs are, you are not in control of your finances.

I'd like to discuss three scenarios for a minute:

1. **You spend more than you earn.** Clearly that is unsustainable for a long period. Excess spending would need to be met from savings or through borrowing. Meeting costs from savings or assets is only sustainable if you have calculated how much you need and made prudent assumptions to ensure it lasts until you are 100 years old; otherwise you risk running out of money. Borrowing is unsustainable in the long term, as

the cost of borrowing will only increase your outgoings further.

2. **Your income meets your expenses and there is no surplus income.** In this scenario, there is no disposable income and no scope to save for the future. If you are in this scenario and working, it is unlikely that financial independence will be achieved as there is no budget for monthly savings. In this scenario, you can meet your costs for as long as you continue to work. When you stop working, you will struggle to meet costs as you have not been able to save all those years. This is sustainable in the short and medium term, but not in the long term.

3. **Your income exceeds your expenses and each month there is a surplus.** Here you have options: you can choose to save or you can choose to spend on lifestyle items and discretionary spending.

Out of the three, one gives you the best chance of achieving financial independence for yourself. Note, however, that all give you some chance, as I go on to discuss. Which of the three best describes your current situation?

Save regularly

Saving is a lifetime habit. Some of you were first introduced to this as a child, with your first piggy bank.

However, unless you were educated properly about the real value of money when you were young, you may have to learn good money habits as an adult.

Over the years of working with individuals and families, the ones who achieve financial independence for themselves have something in common: they save regularly. By allocating some of your income each month to saving, you are adopting the best strategy to accumulate enough money that you become financially independent in the future. Saving something every month, even if it is not a regular, fixed amount, is good, though it will be harder to achieve financial independence that way; and while I discuss here the benefit of regular saving, it is important to caveat this by saying that saving something whenever you can is better than not saving at all.

The chances of you winning the lottery in the UK are 1 in about 45 million. If you run your own business, you may be able to sell that in the future to generate a lump sum. I'll discuss in Chapter 9 some of the considerations for that to happen, and whether the proceeds are likely to be enough.

The fact is that financial independence is best achieved by saving part of your income each and every month. To do this, you need to ensure that you have control over your outgoings and know how much you can afford to commit to saving each month. Treat saving like one of your monthly outgoings and after a couple of months of becoming used to not having that money to spend, you will manage on what you have left after saving. The best strategy for regular saving is ensuring that the same amount of money leaves your bank account each month. That is a habit.

When you try and save a bit here and a bit there, it can be difficult to keep track and increases the likelihood of your habit failing to become properly formed. A well-formed habit is something that you do the same way over and over again. Habits are behaviours on autopilot. If you learned to drive or ride a bike, after going through the pain of learning and failing you reached the point where you could do it without thinking. You may even have experienced driving home and not remembering anything about the journey at all.

It takes time for habits to form: some studies say thirty days and some ninety days. Whichever is right, they both show that there is a commitment to changing the way that you do something and sticking to it. I would say that you probably haven't formed a habit of saving each month after thirty days (probably just one pay day). It is easy to form new habits when we have a reason to want to change. *Your* reason to change your money habits and save each month is a desire to achieve financial independence so you can live the rest of your life on your own terms.

Assets vs liabilities

When you save regularly, you have several options about where to put your money: in the bank, buying shares traded on a stock market, property, collective investment schemes, private equity or commodities.

When I talk about accumulating enough money to be financially independent, I am talking about accumulating assets. I define an asset as something which provides you with a return on your investment: importantly, an income. There is a distinction between income and growth and generating income defines something as a real asset. Let's look at some of the options for investing your money to see whether these meet the test.

Cash in the bank

At the moment interest rates are at historic lows. For the last twelve years, interest rates have remained low and now with a new coronavirus crisis there seems to be no return to 'normal' interest rates. Banks rarely fail, however, so you can probably always get your money out.

Shares

When you buy shares in companies listed on stock exchanges, your return comes in two ways: by increase in the share price (capital growth) and by profit share (dividends). Dividends forms part of your total return and, importantly, you can reinvest your dividends to buy more shares – I explain why this is important in Chapter 6. The price can go down as well as up, dividends can fluctuate and there is no guarantee that you will be able to sell your shares when you want or need to, especially if you invest in unknown, or unquoted, companies.

Property

Property is always a popular investment choice and, since the 1980s, a number of ways to own shares in property have made it easier. It is a physical asset, which some people favour over intangibles such as shares or collective investment schemes. The return on investment can come in two ways: by appreciation in the value of the property over time and by any income that can be generated by renting the property to a tenant. However, property requires maintenance, the costs of which will reduce your overall return. While you will usually be able to sell shares in (say) a property fund, the managers may set terms and conditions on this; and selling a physical property takes time and costs money.

Collective investment schemes

This broad class covers a range of investment structures that have one thing in common, they are run by professional fund managers who invest for you. The range of investment strategies and types is too broad to cover in this book and I wouldn't do it justice to try and summarise. The return from the majority of these schemes does meet my test, in that capital growth can be provided and many generate dividend income or interest income. The price can go down as well as up, dividends/interest can fluctuate and the managers may set terms and conditions on selling units.

Private equity

This has been a popular asset class in recent years, due to increasing availability. Private equity describes investment in companies that have not made their shares publicly available through a listing on the main stock markets. Previously, barriers to entry, such as high investment minimums, made this unavailable for most people. However, several online platforms help investors put their capital into smaller companies looking to grow. The return that investors get from these investments is usually a capital return on a future event for the company. This may be a stock market listing, acquisition or sale of the company. Typically, no dividends are paid during the holding period, which may be fixed: so you may not be able to get your money out sooner (or at all, if the future event does not happen). There is real risk of failure in these investments so they are usually only held by those prepared to risk loss of their entire investment.

Commodities

'Commodities' describes a broad category, covering things needed for other processes (eg precious metals, oil, coffee, wool). Investors can speculate on movements in the prices of commodities through investing into financial instruments that track the price. Most investors who invest in something like gold do not actually buy physical gold but a financial product that tracks the price. During the period you hold these investments, you receive no income. The return comes from selling what you invest in at a higher price in the future and making a capital gain. Because investments into commodities can be complex, a simpler route to investing is via a collective investment scheme investing in commodities. Unlike private equity, your investment cannot fail, but the price can rise and fall very quickly.

Plan for different phases of spending

During your lifetime, the cost of your lifestyle will naturally vary. As we grow and develop, our habits and thoughts change and the things we spend money on may change too. It can be difficult to plan for what you are going to spend in the future, when it is too far away to imagine.

I ask you to consider three phases of spending:

1. The cost of your current lifestyle

2. The cost of the lifestyle you desire in future

3. What your lifestyle will cost in later life

Right now you live a certain lifestyle and your monthly and annual outgoings are made up of essential and non-essential expenses. I would describe an essential expense as something that you have to pay: such as utility bills, for example. Throughout life most of us will always have some essential expenses that we must meet. You will also have non-essential expenditure, things that you pay for each month and year, that you choose to buy. When you add these up you get the cost of your lifestyle as it stands today.

Once you have considered what your current lifestyle costs are, the next step is to think about how your expenses will change when you are financially independent. What would your expenses be each and every month to allow you to live your best life? Use your current lifestyle costs as a base to consider how your spending might change in the future. Your essential costs may not change much. When you think about your future desired lifestyle, factor in all the things that you want to do in life, the things you might be putting off and not doing now. When you are financially independent, if you have planned properly you will be able to do all the things you have always wanted to do, so think big.

There is a point as we get older where we naturally reduce our spending. As health declines, we lose the ability to do certain things we enjoyed when we were younger. As we have already established, time speeds up as you get older and the time when you become less active will creep up on you quickly. This is why it is so important that you plan to do all the things you want to do, while you can do them, so that you don't get to the point where you are unable to do things and look back at missed opportunities. When it comes to planning what this phase of your life will cost, essential outgoings must still be met and there may or may not be any change. Non-essential expenditure may decrease.

Experiences vs stuff

Robert Waldinger is a psychiatrist who works on the Harvard Study of Adult Development, often called the longest study of happiness. In November 2015, Robert spoke at TEDx on the findings of this study.

At the start of the talk, Robert refers to a survey of millennials who were asked what their most important life goals were. Over 80% said that their goal was to get rich and another 50% of the same group said their goal was to become famous. The Harvard Study seeks to answer whether these life goals actually make us happy, and did so by studying a group of 724 men over seventy-five years. During the duration of the study, the researchers asked the participants to answer questions each year on their health, home lives and careers.

Impressively, the study has managed to keep going and sixty of the original participants are still alive and answering questions in their 90s. When the study commenced, it focused on two groups of men: Harvard students who graduated during the Second World War and a group of boys from one of the poorest neighbourhoods in Boston. When the participants were young men, the same age as the millennials in the survey Waldinger referred to, they had the same goals: to become rich and famous. The researchers have followed the many different paths of these men since 1945, through their careers, health issues and social status. The participants were interviewed about their lives throughout, and asked to supply medical records including blood and brain scans.

The findings are important: what will most affect our happiness, how long we live and our health is the quality of the relationships we have. Those with strong family and social connections live happier, longer lives. Loneliness has exactly the opposite effect, resulting in declining brain structure, lower satisfaction with life and earlier death. The study found that you can be lonely and also have friends and family around you, so the quality of those relationships is crucial. Toxic relationships are bad for us; good-quality relationships will give you the most fulfilment in life, keeping you healthy, both physically and mentally, for longer.

In September 2010, Daniel Kahneman and Angus Deaton published a research article on the effects of income on wellbeing.[11] The study involved more than 450,000 respondents to a daily survey conducted by the Gallup Organisation and produced the Gallup-Heathways Well Being Index. The question that they wanted to answer with their research was 'does money buy happiness?' Before doing so, they had to define how they were going to interpret happiness, as it is a broad emotion. They broke it down into two categories that they could measure: emotional wellbeing and life evaluation. Emotional wellbeing covers the frequency and intensity of our experiences with joy, stress, sadness, anger and affection. Life evaluation refers to the thoughts people have about their lives, when they think about it.

To assess the role that money plays, Kahneman and Deaton used income as a measure. What they noticed is that emotional wellbeing increases as income increases. This makes sense, as low income can mean money problems. Money problems can contribute

---

11 Daniel Kahneman and Angus Deaton, 'High income improves evaluation of life but not emotional well-being', *Proceedings of the National Academy of Sciences of the USA*, 107/38 (2010).

greatly to our overall stress levels, and difficult decisions can result in conflict with others, increase in sadness and reduction in joy and affection. The intensity of the stress and sadness could increase with lower income levels. Put simply, low income is miserable.

The relationship between emotional wellbeing and income is not linear, though: emotional wellbeing flattens out when a household income moves above $75,000 (in 2010 terms). This means that there is a point at which earning more money doesn't translate into greater happiness. Once our basic financial needs are met and we feel no stress about money, our emotional wellbeing plateaus.

In contrast, there is a linear relationship between income and the quality of the thoughts that people have about their lives. As income levels increase, the quality of our life experiences increases: effectively, we have more freedom to do things that are important to us and have experiences that we value.

What these two studies tell us is that we can maximise our happiness by doing things we love, with people that are important to us, by deepening our relationships with our friends and family through sharing experiences. To give an example, one of my most memorable experiences in recent years was a trip I took with my wife and father to Monet's house and gardens in Giverny, France. We made a last-minute plan, one week, to book an early-weekend train to France and drove to the gardens for the day. This day out was not particularly costly (a Channel Tunnel return ticket, fuel for the car, lunch for three and entry tickets), but the memories of that day and the photos we took will stay with me for the rest of my life. We talk about it often and fondly. The quality of the experience was high, compared to the cost, and I am certain that it contributed more to my happiness and wellbeing than had I spent the money unwisely.

The best use of your money, to increase your happiness, is on memorable experiences that increase the quality of your relationships with the people most important to you.

5

Behavioural Finance

I was first introduced to behavioural finance while studying for an investment exam. I quickly learned that I had made many behavioural errors in managing my own investments up until that point, without even being aware of it. It was a sobering lesson to learn. As I read through the list of different ways that our own investor behaviours can lure us into making poor decisions, I realised I had been guilty of most of them at some point. At this time, I was managing my own pension portfolio on an investment platform, and thought I was doing a good job of it. I wasn't.

It's not always easy to make good decisions about money and in fact, far from it. We are often trying to make decisions about our future, which can be emotional, while dealing with complex information.

In this chapter I am going to cover some of the main areas that relate specifically to making investment decisions. If financial independence is your goal, making poor investment choices along the way can really harm your chances of achieving it.

Warren Buffett is often quoted as having said that, when he passes away, his will states that his wife is to invest her money in index-tracking funds. These are investment schemes that track the performance of an index, and don't depend on a fund manager actively picking stocks. Warren Buffett is one of the best-known, most successful active investors in history. He was taught at Columbia University by Benjamin Graham, who wrote *The Intelligent Investor*. Buffett's investment style is called 'value investing', which means seeking out companies that are undervalued at the moment and purchasing them on the basis that over time a return will be made. He has stated his strategy is to buy companies that he thinks will last long into the future, and never sell them.

Warren Buffett is known to spend up to 80% of his day reading. He is quoted as saying that one of the secrets to his success is 'going to bed a little smarter each day'. Buffett is also of the opinion that the law of compound returns also applies to knowledge. Spending so much time reading and researching, he will not invest in a company until he knows everything he can find out about it. Then, only at the point where he is convinced that he is making the right decision, will he invest. This process means that few investments are made and there is little turnover in his portfolio.

When Warren Buffett says that his wife is to invest in index trackers only, it is because he is well aware of how difficult investment decisions are. Many people have tried to beat the market and failed, through poor behaviours leading to bad decisions. The lesson from Warren Buffett is, if you are going to manage your own investments, be at peace with the fact that there is a near-certainty of getting it wrong.

Heuristics

Heuristics are mental rules of thumb, shortcuts in our decision-making. We need rules of thumb to make decisions; without them we would have to think through, in detail, every decision we make during the day. Some are helpful, like the 'Rule of 72' I will discuss in Chapter 6. The 'Rule of 72' is a way of working out compound returns. It is not 100% accurate, which is exactly what makes it a rule of thumb. Its purpose is to help us work something out quickly. Heuristics can also be described as educated guesses, or when we make a decision based on a feeling we have.

EXERCISE

Consider this problem:

'A bat and a ball together cost £1.10. The bat costs £1 more than the ball. How much does the ball cost?'

If you answered £0.10, you answered incorrectly. When you think about it harder, it can't be £0.10. If the ball costs £0.10 and the bat costs £1 more, then the two added together would be £1.20.

The correct answer is that the ball costs £0.05, meaning the bat costs £1.05 and the two added together give you £1.10.

This problem is often cited when it comes to the difference between making a quick decision and taking your time to ensure that the decision is right. Psychologist Daniel Kahneman attributes this to what he calls system 1 and system 2 decision-making. System 1 leads to quicker, more intuitive decisions, whereas system 2 requires far more analysis and consideration of information before coming to a decision.[12] So if you answered £0.10 to the question above, it may have been because intuitively it just sounded like the right answer.

We use heuristics all the time; about 95% of our daily decisions are made using them. If we had to take our time with every decision, we wouldn't get much done.

---

12   Daniel Kahneman, 'Of 2 minds: How fast and slow thinking shape perception and choice', *Scientific American*, 15 June 2012.

Heuristics allow us to generalise, approximate and find shortcuts. If you drive a car and have done for a while, you may have experienced driving somewhere and arriving at your destination without remembering much about the journey. You didn't have to think through every single action in detail; it is almost as if some internal autopilot took over.

Heuristics are important to understand when making financial decisions. We can generalise, approximate and sometimes take a short cut, but at other times a short cut can mean missing an important detail, a detail which could be the difference between a good decision and a bad one. Even more importantly, our reliance on heuristics increases when we are under stress, feeling emotional, when the information is complex or if we have little time. When there is too much information on offer, investors can be faced with choice overload. This leads to procrastination, and sometimes no decision is made for fear of making a wrong one.

Where given choice, more than 90% of UK occupational pension scheme members invest in the default investment fund. Even where offered many funds and portfolios to choose from, few ever change from the default option that was selected for them by their employer or pension scheme provider. The lack of understanding about how pensions work, coupled with the amount of information available on fund choices, makes most people opt to do nothing, as the simplest choice. In my experience, few people understand their workplace pension or have taken the time to investigate how it works and what their options are.

Herd mentality

The first shares I ever bought were in a company called Northern Rock; you may have heard of them. Northern Rock was a bank listed on the UK stock exchange and, as the banking crisis started developing in September 2007, they were refused liquidity support from the Bank of England. The share price crashed in the resulting panic, which within twenty-four hours saw the public queuing up to withdraw their money from branches.

At the time I worked for a bank, in the administration team of their regulated complaints department. During the crisis, a helpful chap wandered past my desk and told me and a colleague that Northern Rock shares were a bargain and he had bought some. He told us how the quality of their outstanding mortgage book was excellent, and that once all this nonsense was over the share price would rebound. At that time it had fallen about 90% from its pre-crisis level and, if the share price did return to normal, the upside was huge. I excitedly got on the phone, opened a stock-broking account and placed my first telephone trade for £200 of Northern Rock shares. The dealing fee over the phone was something like £25, which thinking about it now should have been a red flag. However, I was sold on the story and only saw the upside at this point.

What happened next is the start of the global banking crisis that saw global markets plunging around the world, central banks bailing out the economy and a recession that we still have not fully recovered from. Northern Rock were nationalised in February 2008, a mere five months after I bought the shares. So the first investment I ever made, on a 'tip' from a mature colleague who, to me, seemed to know what he was talking about, was a complete failure. Whether we like to believe it or not, the fact is, we are influenced by what others around us do. When it comes to making investment decisions, this is worth being aware of, as I found out the hard way. The driving force behind my decision to invest was greed. At the time, I wasn't earning a great deal and the opportunity to make money quickly blinded me to the risks.

Financial markets are complex and difficult to understand because of the number of participants, the terms of financial instruments and the volume of information available. However, they can be simply understood through the principle of supply and demand. On any given day, are there more buyers for a company's shares, or more sellers? If there are more buyers than sellers the price may rise, and if there are more sellers than buyers the price may fall. It's a highly simplistic way of looking at the stock market, but helpful in understanding the effect of herd mentality on markets.

Between May and December 2017, the price of Bitcoin soared from around $2,000 to $19,000. At the time, the rise of the Bitcoin price was frequently mentioned in the press and the financial pages. Stories came out of 'Bitcoin millionaires', and there was a rush of registrations for Bitcoin wallets as people tried to grab their slice of the profits. In five days at the end of December the price fell by a third and by February 2018 it had fallen a further 50%. At the end of December 2018, the price was back down to $3,000. This is a financial instrument that is unregulated, backed by no central bank and has been plagued by a series of high-profile thefts. The only explanation I can see for the dramatic rise and fall is the mentality of the herd.

As the price of an asset is driven upwards by an increased number of buyers, more buyers join in, in the hope of achieving high returns. This greed pushes the price higher still, until the point where the early speculators decide to take profits. Once the tide turns, more and more holders turn into sellers. The price rose all the way to $19,000, meaning that at that point and just before it there were more buyers than sellers. These investors may have been the first to sell in a panic when the price started to fall rapidly. Many have never recovered the losses they incurred in the space of those few days, weeks or months.

When making decisions, we can be biased by the limits to the knowledge we have. This is called the availability heuristic. When you think of how probable different causes of death are, things like shark attacks often seem more likely than they actually are. Shark attacks are newsworthy. If a surfer gets attacked by a shark, it hits the media around the world. However, each year around the world about four people die from shark attacks, while champagne corks, falling out of bed and cows are all far more likely to kill you. Due to the availability heuristic, you are likely to perceive a greater risk from shark attacks as they are more newsworthy. There are also fewer blockbuster films about killer cows to worry you. The point is, our decision-making can be biased towards what we are already familiar with.

In recent months, while I have been writing this, we have been in lockdown owing to COVID-19. Working from home has brought its challenges as well as its benefits. One of the factors that enables me to continue to operate a business is having access to virtual meeting software. Like many other business owners, the two types that I have been using have been Microsoft Teams and Zoom. Microsoft saw a 30% uplift in their share price from a low at the end of March 2020 to the beginning of June. Zoom has seen their share price rise about 52% over the same period. The stock ticker for Zoom Video Communications Inc is NASDAQ: ZM.

There also happens to be a completely unrelated company called Zoom Technologies (ticker ZOOM), whose share price rocketed to a peak 180 times its January 2020 price before trading was suspended on 8 April. Investors had been buying the wrong company, owing to confusion over the stock ticker. On the face of it, if you log on to your trading account wanting to buy Zoom shares and you buy Zoom shares, what is there to question? This is a straightforward example of heuristic decision-making.

The price of Zoom Technologies hit its peak and then rapidly started falling as investors started to realise their mistake. As more investors turned to sellers, panic set in and the US Securities and Exchange Commission (SEC) suspended trading. The reason trading was suspended is that, now investors were aware of the error, many would sell, sending the share price plunging. With trading suspended, this has only been delayed. It is inevitable that, once trading resumes, investors who realise their error will look to sell, many suffering significant losses. The suspension means that the price correction *might* be slower than it was when the panic was at its height, so Zoom Technologies *might* survive.

Just as greed can motivate us to buy, fear can motivate us to sell.

Loss aversion and gambler's fallacy

Investors act illogically at the best of times, but this is exemplified when losses are made. The initial emotional reaction to seeing a fall in the value of your investments is fear. Fear is a powerful emotion and when it comes to making investments, there is greater emotion attached to a loss than there is to an equal gain. Where greed may blind us to risks and make us overconfident, fear can be more damaging.

Emotions are instincts and we have seven primary emotions: contempt, happiness, sadness, anger, disgust, surprise and fear. Our emotions are triggered by external stimuli and have developed to create an instinctive reaction. These reactions may be to protect us, or for social interaction, and they have evolved over the time that humans have been on this planet. An instinct is an unconscious reaction: it happens without our control and we become consciously aware of it after. If someone smiles at you, you can't help but smile back. Laughter is said to be infectious. If you have children, you may have noticed different emotions on their faces when they were babies. Greed isn't an emotion, it's a character trait. We learn how to be greedy; it is a habit that is developed. Fear is an emotion, designed to create an instinctive reaction and that can be problematic for investors.

The part of your brain that is activated when fear sets in is the amygdala. The amygdala's normal reaction to fear is the flight or fight response. Our brain is designed to react and respond quickly to danger, which for investors can mean an initial emotional reaction: usually, to press the sell button to protect from further losses. Problems arise when decisions are made emotionally rather than rationally. Selling in a falling market may feel like the right thing to do at the time, but what if the downturn is short-lasting and you have potentially acted too early?

Data collected between 20 February and 15 May 2020 by Fidelity Investments[13] showed that around 18% of their account holders sold all their stocks at some point between those dates. When they broke the data down by age group, that figure increased to just over 30% of over-65s. This age group have been investing for long enough to have experienced the last two market shocks in 2008/09 and 2000/03. Yet, nearly a third of the most experienced have made a behavioural error by selling their entire portfolios. Research by Schroders[14] showed that if in 2008 you had sold your portfolio after a 49% fall in the US market and put your money in cash, by April 2020 you would still not have recovered your losses. Whereas, had you stayed invested you would have recovered your losses in 4.8

13 See www.fa-mag.com/news/33--of-investors-over-65-sold-all-their-stocks-this-year-56400.html.
14 See www.schroders.com/en/insights/economics/downturns-this-deep-can-take-a-long-time-to-recover-from-financially-and-mentally

years and gone on to average 7.4% per annum over the same period.

Our experiences with loss can also affect the decisions we make in the future. The phrase 'once bitten, twice shy' is relevant in a lot of cases where investors have been spooked by falls in their investments and reacted by selling. The experience can be enough to put some investors off ever wanting to go through it again. Over the years I have met many people who invested right before the Dot Com Crash in 1999/2000, who have never returned to investing in the stock market. This is a terrific shame, as later on I will discuss the effect inflation can have on your money and why investing offers a hedge against it.

Gambler's fallacy describes the belief that, if a pattern in one direction can be observed, then in future there is higher likelihood that the pattern will reverse, or that the position will even out. For example, if I tossed a coin ten times and each of those ten times it landed on heads, would you expect the next result to be tails? Statistically, the chances of it being tails remains 50%. We can be drawn into thinking that there is no way this streak of results can continue – at some point it has to be tails, of course, but a coin has no memory so the previous results do not affect the chances of the result of the next toss.

This belief shows in investors who decide to invest in a company based on a recent fall or rise in the share price. Investing because a share price has fallen could be perceived as a bargain: the recent fall could be a run of bad luck. On the other side, investors may see a share price rise rapidly and think that they can ride this momentum higher. The problem is that both cases are illogical, yet many investors fall for them. Trading platforms don't help either; a number of them publish on their websites today's biggest winners and losers; or most viewed; or most traded (herd mentality).

Overconfidence

Until the beginning of 2020, global stock markets saw a period of growth since the bank crisis of 2008/09. Many investors who started investing during these years will not have experienced the shock and panic of a market crash and economic recession. In this environment, it is easy to become overconfident in your investing abilities. When I managed my own investment portfolio, I drew a lot of confidence from the fact that I had passed exams in investment management and had an investment process. The reality was, I didn't give my research and investment process anywhere near the dedication and detail it required. I was making quite decent returns, but a rising tide raises all ships and I was probably making about the same return as the market.

When we believe strongly in something, we take in information that supports our belief, and throw away what doesn't fit. Horoscopes are written so vaguely that what they say could apply to anyone reading them, and those who believe in them apply what fits and throw away the rest. We are biased by what we believe, and once our opinions form they can be hard to change. When it comes to investing, this can mean we choose to remember, and place more importance on, the winning investments we made, forgetting the losers. This can lead to overconfidence and that can lead to poor risk management.

Trying to time the market can be costly. Investors who save the same amount of money each month, with a long-term plan in place, have a higher success rate. The problem with trying to time the market, guessing when it might reach its peak or bottom, is that we are just not good at it. As markets fall, those who exit the market try to time their re-entry. Most miss the recovery, and since some of the best returns are made in the first few days, this means poor returns. A study by DALBAR, Inc[15] showed that between 1996 and 2015 average investor returns were 5.19% per annum, against 9.85% per annum returned by the S&P 500.

Investors who save each month, with a long-term plan, don't have the problem of trying to time their investments. As investments are made monthly, low and high prices average out. This is called pound-cost averaging, and it increases your chances of beating the returns of those who try to guess where the market

---

15 See www.thebalance.com/why-average-investors-earn-below-average-market-returns-2388519

will move next. I show how this works later in this chapter.

Concentrations and diversification

We invest in what we are familiar with, which means that UK investors tend to have a bias towards UK companies. Remember the availability heuristic: we are more likely to invest in companies we have heard of before.

When investing in company shares, investors face two main risks: *market risk* and *specific risk*. Market risk is the risk that comes with being invested; the general trend of the market will affect the share price of the company you invest in. In a market crash, nearly all shares are likely to suffer falls. You cannot do much about market risk, and it doesn't matter how many shares you hold. Portfolios invested in a small number of companies not only carry the risk that they will rise and fall to some degree as the market does, but carry a greater risk should any of the individual companies face problems: specific risk. This can be reduced by diversification. Typically, a portfolio holding more than twenty shares is much less risky than one holding fewer.

Most investors who manage their own portfolios hold fewer than twenty shares. Concentrations can occur not just by holding shares in too few companies, but by not achieving sufficient diversity across different sectors of the economy. Collective investment schemes can offer diversity to small savings pots. Warren Buffett is famously in favour of highly concentrated portfolios, but as I mentioned earlier in this chapter he doesn't invest until he is absolutely convinced there are reasons to do so. In his opinion, being highly concentrated means that you take your research far more seriously.

The blend of asset classes (property, shares, bonds, commodities etc) within a portfolio is responsible for the bulk of investment returns. Stock picking does not add anywhere near as much to your return as having the right asset mix. The asset mix you choose may be responsible for around 85% of your total return. The right asset mix will also help manage the amount of risk that you face.

If you work with a professional portfolio manager, they will select an asset mix based on your circumstances and the level of risk you are prepared to take. The different risk levels represent your level of exposure to potential losses. As risk and return are related, you give up (some) potential for growth in return for (some) protection against losses. Example portfolios are below to show what the asset mix might be at different levels (this is an example for illustrative purposes only):

Asset mix (%)	Conservative	Balanced	Growth
UK equities	17.5	30	32.5
International equities	15	32.5	45
Bonds	37.5	17.5	7.5
Cash	5	5	2.5
Property	5	5	5
Alternatives	20	10	7.5
Total	100	100	100

This table shows different sample portfolios for cautious, medium-risk and high-risk investors. The main trade-off that you can see is between equities (company shares) and bonds (different types of debt issued by companies and governments). In this example equities are broken down into UK and international, and could be broken down further into large, medium and small companies. In the UK, indices that track companies include the FTSE 100, which represents the largest 100 companies by market capitalisation (number of shares in issue multiplied by the share price), the FTSE 250, the next-largest 250 companies, and the FTSE Allshare (all quoted companies). A wide range of other indices break this down further, such as by business sector.

Bonds are a wide range of different types of debt issued by companies and governments. When companies want to raise money, they can sell bonds that pay interest, at fixed intervals and a fixed interest rate until a maturity date when the bond is bought back by the company. Governments do the same – UK government bonds are called gilts. The main thing to remember is that companies (and governments) with poor credit ratings have to pay higher interest: the risk of companies (and governments) not repaying their debts is reflected in the rate at which they can borrow money.

Cash may be 'money in the bank', but is more likely to be financial instruments that track interest rate changes. We discussed property and a range of other investments ('alternatives') in Chapter 4.

Bonds are seen as less risky than shares, which is why lower-risk portfolios will often contain more of them. To some extent, bonds and shares are negatively correlated: when one goes down, the other goes up. In diversifying your portfolio to reduce risk, that is ideal as when one asset class is falling the other should be rising to compensate. The classic example explaining this is umbrellas and ice cream: when it's raining you would expect to see higher umbrella sales and lower ice cream sales. When the sun is out the opposite occurs. However, it can't be predicted from one year to the next which asset class will perform best, so it pays to have a broad exposure.

This broad exposure could be achieved by investing in different asset classes, across different countries (eg developed and emerging), across different business sectors, in companies of different sizes and, in the case of investment funds, with different investment managers, working for different companies and with different investment strategies and market views.

A professional portfolio manager will blend all these asset classes into a mix, using methodology that looks to strike the best balance between the degree of risk you are comfortable with and the return you would like to earn. Private investors find this hard to do as the research and technology isn't available to amateurs. However, investors have a wide range of investment options available where this is done for them – leaving them in charge of picking the portfolio that best fits their circumstances.

Anchoring

When trying to predict the future, investors can hold reference points which impact the prediction they make. A common anchor (reference point) is the price at which an investor bought a share.

If the investment fell after purchase, the investor may be tempted to keep holding onto it until they have at least made up their losses. Without further analysis to appraise the reasons behind a fall in share prices, investors can end up holding losing stocks for longer than they should. Holding onto losing stocks too long can also be explained by the avoidance of regret. Since selling a share that has fallen means acknowledging a loss, and therefore a bad investment, investors can be tempted to hold on in hope. Staying invested to avoid admitting a mistake has been made is called 'regret aversion'. The logical thing to do is think about whether there is still value in holding the company, or whether other factors behind a fall mean selling is the right decision, even at a loss.

Investors can also act irrationally when it comes to taking profits. There is far more emotion attached to a loss, but that does not mean that no errors in logical judgement occur when gains are made. A common behaviour is selling too early. Investors see profits and worry about losing them. The higher price that has been achieved becomes a new anchor, and any fall from that price is seen as 'loss' even though the investment might still be worth more than you paid for it.

Mental accounting

Economist Richard Thaler developed the concept of mental accounting in 1999. He found that people place different values on money, and apply differing criteria, when all money should be treated the same.[16] This concept explains why some investors place a higher importance on investing for the medium to long term, while having high-interest debt such as credit cards. The logical thing to do would be pay off the expensive debt first, and after that start investing.

If there is something that you want to buy, but you feel guilty about spending the money, you can use

16 Richard Thaler, 'Mental accounting matters', *Journal of Behavioral Decision Making*, 12 (1999).

mental accounting to your advantage. If you set up a savings account with the specific purpose of building up the money needed for the purchase, you will feel less guilty about spending the money when you have reached your target. As you have already accounted for the spending, there is less guilt attached.

Advice

As we near the end of this chapter, you will have realised that there are many biases that can influence the decisions you make and, when it comes to investing, this can impact your ability to build up assets effectively in the long term. To mitigate the risk of making poor financial decisions, you can either choose to manage your own investments while being highly aware of your own biases; or decide that you are not confident enough of remaining unbiased and delegate the management of your investments to a professional.

I chose the second option, but not just because I work in financial services. I started studying behavioural finance six years ago (2014) when I was working for my qualification with the Chartered Institute for Securities and Investment (Chartered Wealth Manager). This is a Masters-level qualification designed for wealth managers and gives holders highly detailed knowledge and the skills to manage investment portfolios. The fact that I had more experience and knowledge than most investors only led to a greater degree of overconfidence. After studying behavioural finance, I came to the conclusion that, when I looked back at my own history of investing, I had made many poor decisions due to biases. From that point onwards I decided to delegate the management of my investments to professional fund managers.

Each year the US investment and advisory firm Charles Schwab publish data on their client accounts. Some of these are brokerage accounts and some are advised accounts, where investment decisions are not made by the account holder. In the 2019 report, the average balance of self-traded accounts was $234,673 vs $448,515 for advised accounts.[17] There are other reasons for the difference than behaviours, however. I have worked with people who started as DIY investors and then reached a point where they had enough money and were then worried about making a wrong decision. DIY investors tend to invest lower amounts as they may not be able to afford an adviser, or may be cost-conscious. Investors with larger portfolios may be time-poor and have a higher likelihood of delegating.

Behaviours do account for some of the differences between the average balances. Poor market timing and overtrading can impact returns that DIY investors make. Behavioural economist Meir Statman refers in his book *What Investors Really Want* to a Swedish study which found that the heaviest traders lose 4% of their account each year to dealing fees, price spreads and market timing.

---

17   Charles Schwab Corporation, *2019 Annual Report.*

Pound-cost averaging and value averaging

When you invest monthly, whether in shares or a collective investment scheme, the price at which you invest will change. Each month the price will rise or fall. This means that, over time, the unit or share price at which you invest tends to average out. This effect is called pound-cost averaging.

EXAMPLE

Invest £100 each month into a fund with a starting price of £1 per unit.

Month	Invested	Price	Units	Total units
1	£100	£1	100	100
2	£100	£1.05	95	195
3	£100	£0.98	102	297
4	£100	£0.95	105	403
5	£100	£1.02	98	501
6	£100	£1.08	93	593
7	£100	£1.15	87	680
8	£100	£1.12	89	769
9	£100	£1.11	90	860
10	£100	£1.17	85	945
11	£100	£1.20	83	1,028
12	£100	£1.17	85	1,114

Note: Units purchased are rounded to nearest whole unit, to keep the maths simple.

Total number of 1,114 units purchased at an average price of £0.93.

This averaging effect helps smooth the rises and falls in the unit price throughout the year. Saving monthly this way reduces the temptation to try timing the market. If you invest the same each month, you do not need to worry about market timing at all. Some months you will buy more units and others less.

However, pound-cost averaging becomes inefficient if you have a lump sum you want to invest; instead you should use a technique called value averaging. This works by specifying the number of months over which you want to invest, and then aiming to increase the value of your investment each month to a fixed amount. Rather than investing the same amount each time, you invest more when prices are lower and less when they are higher.

EXAMPLE

Let's use a sum of £100,000 that you would like to invest over the next four months. Each month you will increase the value of your investment by £25,000. Unit price is again £1 at the start.

Month 1

£25,000 is invested at £1 per unit. So, we have 25,000 units valued at £1

Month 2

The unit price has risen to £1.20, so the 25,000 units already owned are now worth £30,000. This month £20,000 is invested, to increase total value to £50,000, buying 16,666 units. Units now total 41,666.

Month 3

The unit price has fallen to £0.85, so the units owned are now worth £35,416. This month £39,584 is invested to increase total value to £75,000, buying 46,569 units. Total units are now 88,235.

Month 4

In the last month the unit price is £1.10, making the total portfolio worth £97,058. In this month the last £15,416 will be invested, purchasing 14,014 units for a total of 102,249, worth £112,473.

Conclusion

If pound-cost averaging had been used, then the average unit price would have been £0.98, purchasing 97,971 units worth £107,768. In this case, value averaging has performed better.

6

Compounding

'Compound interest is the eighth wonder of the world.
He who understands it earns it... he who doesn't...
pays it.'
— Unknown[18]

Compounding is the most important concept to understand when you save and invest. Specifically, it means potentially exponential growth in the future. Compound growth can seem unimportant at first and many people sell an investment before they see the exponential effects. To start with, I'll explain some terms. Simple interest describes a return you receive on your initial investment (the principal). Compounding is earning interest on *both* the principal *and* all the interest you have already earned.

---

18   https://quoteinvestigator.com/2019/09/09/interest/, accessed 20 July 2020.

COMPOUNDING FORMULA

Annual: $A = P(1 + r)^t$

More frequently than annual: $A = P(1 + r/n)^{nt}$

A = amount

P = principal, your initial investment

r = rate of interest

n = number of times interest is compounded per unit of t (eg if monthly, $n = 12$)

t = time, a round number, usually years

Let's look at some examples to explain the difference between simple and compound interest. In these examples, I'll use an initial investment of £1,000, a return of 5% per annum, annual compounding and holding the investment for five years (the 'term').

Year	Simple interest		Compound interest	
	Interest	Subtotal	Interest	Subtotal
1	£1,000 × 5% = £50	£1,050	£1,000 × 5% = £50	£1,050
2	£1,000 × 5% = £50	£1,100	£1,050 × 5% = £52.50	£1,102.50
3	£1,000 × 5% = £50	£1,150	£1,102.50 × 5% = £55.13	£1,157.63
4	£1,000 × 5% = £50	£1,200	£1,157.63 × 5% = £57.87	£1,215.50
5	£1,000 × 5% = £50	£1,250	£1,215.50 × 5% = £60.78	£1,276.28

Compounding has added an extra £26.28. Run the same calculation forward thirty years and using simple interest your initial investment would now be worth £2,500, a gain of £1,500. With compounding your total balance would be £4,321.94, a gain of £3,321.94 – more than double the return from simple interest.

How often compounding applies has an impact on the overall return that you receive. Compounding the same rate more often will increase the overall return and compounding it less often will decrease the return. If I had compounded monthly (not 5% per month, but an annual equivalent rate – AER – of 5%, compounded monthly), after thirty years the return would have been £3,467.74.

Banks and lenders usually apply the frequency of compounding to work in their favour, not yours. Savings accounts paying interest often compound less often than (say) your mortgage. It is not uncommon to see debt compounded daily and yet savings compounded monthly or less frequently.

So far I've illustrated how compounding works on a lump-sum investment, but what if you are saving regularly? The formula for that is:

$$FV = PMT \times \frac{(1 + r/n)^{nt} - 1}{r/n}$$

where r, n and t have the same meanings as before, and

FV = future value

PMT = monthly payment

EXAMPLE

Let's say you invest £100 per month at 5% annual return for five years:

$r = 0.05$

$n = 12$ (we are making monthly payments, so twelve months is twelve payments)

$t = 5$

$PMT = £100$

$$FV = £100 \times \frac{(1 + 0.05/12)^{60} - 1}{0.05/12}$$

$$= £100 \times \frac{1.00416^{60} - 1}{0.00416}$$

$$= £100 \times 0.28336 / 0.00416$$

$$= £100 \times 68.0061$$

$$= £6,800.61$$

The total contributions were £6,000, meaning growth of £800.61 has been achieved.

That might not sound that exciting, and certainly if you have been committed to investing diligently every month for the last five years, you might feel you haven't made much progress. This is where some people stop, as progress seems slow, so what is the point of continuing? As already mentioned, compounding has an exponential effect. If I run this calculation forward thirty years, the total amount built up is £83,225.86, over which period your savings contributions total £36,000, meaning the growth is £47,225.86. Run forward forty years, and the total is £152,602.02, your contributions total £48,000, so growth is £104,602.02. The additional ten years (forty years' savings, not thirty) costs an additional £12,000 in contributions, but the growth is more than double. These formulas can be set up in an Excel spreadsheet for those of you who know your way around spreadsheets.

Saving monthly is a lifetime habit and starting early provides the greatest benefit further down the line. Another way to look at the difference between a thirty-year and a forty-year term is to consider the cost of delay. Deciding to delay saving by ten years doesn't mean you miss out on the return over the *first* ten years, it means you miss out on the return of the *last* ten years, when in the example your savings more than doubled in value. In this case, a costly mistake.

Not only does delaying getting started mean a loss of potential growth later on, it also means that you need to save far more to accumulate the same amount of money. Going back to the above example – saving £100 a month – let's say you knew that you needed to accumulate £83,000 or so over the next thirty years. However, instead of getting started you decide to delay for ten years, leaving twenty years to save the same amount. At the same 5% growth rate, each month you would need to save £202.48 to reach your target – more than double what you would need to save if you started ten years earlier.

Paradoxically, the best time to start saving is as early as you can, which generally means when you have the least available to invest. Starting in your early 20s makes a big difference compared to starting later on. However, starting to save in your early 20s is hard. Firstly, starting salaries are low and there are so many other demands for what money is available. At this time in life, you are finding your place in society which means far more socialising. As mentioned earlier, 'keeping up with the Joneses' happens online now and at a young age the need to compete to fit in is strong. Student debt can be costly for young people too and saving for a house can feel like an impossible task. Squeezing in saving among all this is hard, but it will pay off in the long term. Funnily enough, I remember my early 20s as the time that I had the most fun, with the least amount of money – and that was down to the people I spent my time with.

Money has a value today, and a value in the future. It has a 'time value', which means that what you spend today has a cost in terms of opportunities lost later. The lost opportunity is what you might have been able to do with that money in the future, given its potential to be of greater value (because of compound interest). This is a useful way of thinking when implementing a strategy to evaluate impulse purchases. The money you spend today is robbing your future self of an opportunity to do something with it – and that something might be more important to you. The £50 you spend today on a pleasant but not memorable meal could be part of an amazing holiday in twenty years' time.

The rule of 72

I spoke about rules of thumb in Chapter 5 – heuristics, as they are called. These are mental shortcuts that we use when making decisions, and they can be useful. If you want to know how long it will take for your initial investment to double in value, you can use a simple heuristic called the rule of 72, a short cut to working out compound interest. It allows you to quickly work out compound returns in your head.

The way the rule works is that you divide 72 by the number of years by which you want to double your original investment. The answer you get is the return you would need. As an example, if you wanted to double your initial investment in ten years, you would divide 72 by 10 and get to a required return of 7.2%

per annum; in five years, 14.4%; in twenty years, 3.6%. The average annual return for the FTSE Allshare index over the last 100 years is around 7%.

Where would you use this? This quick shortcut will let you work out the future value of your money at a particular growth rate. This is handy if you are considering making a purchase and want a sense check to see if it is the right thing to do. Delaying purchases and managing your spending so that you can accumulate wealth has already been covered, and delaying gratification can be hard to do.

EXAMPLE

Imagine you have been saving diligently for a few years and have managed to accumulate a fund of £10,000. You need a new car and you are considering using your savings towards the purchase. A quick rule of thumb would say that, if you assumed your savings will grow at 7.2% per annum, then in ten years your £10,000 would double to £20,000 (ignoring any additional savings). In twenty years your £10,000 would become £40,000 and in thirty years it would become £80,000. After ten years your car would have depreciated in value – let's say you buy it for £10,000 and after ten years it is worth £2,000. Over the same ten years, the difference between the potential value of your savings and the value of the car is £18,000. After twenty and thirty years the gap widens (assuming the car still has a value). If your aim is to accumulate wealth and become financially independent, being able to quickly work out the future value of your money at a given growth rate is a good way of helping you avoid impulse purchases.

The way to get round this is to use mental accounting (see Chapter 5). Set up a savings account specifically to fund a car, and then you can feel less guilty about opportunity cost.

Reinvest your dividends

One of the best ways to leverage compounding is to purchase shares and reinvest your dividends. You don't necessarily have to buy shares directly; you can buy an investment fund that will compound for you. When you buy investment funds you usually have a choice between accumulation units which reinvest dividends for you, and income units which pay the dividends to you.

If you own shares and reinvest your dividends, each dividend buys more shares for you. Since dividends are calculated as a percentage of profits per individual share, the more shares you hold then the larger the payment. So, if each year you use your dividends to buy more shares, you will be entitled to a bigger share of next year's dividend pool and if you keep repeating then the effects of compounding will work for you. Many companies offer an automatic dividend reinvestment plan.

The share price may increase over time as well, meaning that not only will there be a return from the dividend payments you receive, but also the growth in the share price. To consider how powerful reinvestment of dividends is, let's look at an example.

On 31 December 1999 the FTSE 100 index was at 6,930. Nineteen years later it stood at 6,845. If you take these figures alone, you might think that over those nineteen years investors made a loss. However, Schroders have calculated that over this period dividends returned 93.5%.[19]

Remember costs and inflation

In the examples earlier in the chapter, the amounts accumulated at the end of thirty or forty years of regular saving seem impressive. However, it is important to remember that, in the future, the value of money will not be what it is today. Over time prices tend to rise steadily, and this is healthy in a normal economy. The UK government has a target of 2% per annum for inflation.

In the forty-year example we looked at, in the end you would have an investment balance of £152,602.02. This balance is in today's money, and in the future will not buy the same amount of goods or services as you

---

19   Schroders, Refinitiv data for FTSE 100, correct at 13 December 2018. Returns not adjusted for inflation or charges.

could today. Inflation needs to be taken into account when working out the growth rate you need to accumulate enough money for the future. In our example, if £152,602.02 was reduced by 2% per year for forty years, in today's terms it would be worth £69,111.99: 2% per year inflation over forty years would erode over half of the value.

Any costs that you incur through investing will also erode the value of your funds in the future. A management fee of 1% a year in the same example would mean that a 5% growth rate would be reduced to 4%. Using the same calculation, that would mean a fund value at the end of £118,196.13. Costs for investment management or advice will reduce the rate of return you earn, and cost could add up over the long term.

Professional advice can be extremely valuable, firstly to avoid a costly delay in getting started, and secondly to help you avoid making behavioural errors. Having an adviser acting as your guide can help motivate you to begin saving and help you on your journey. The cost of delay between thirty and forty years was a difference of £69,376.16. Paying for advice may mean you don't delay getting started, and that is clearly worth it. If studies have shown that on average investors lose 4% per annum by being behaviourally inefficient (see Chapter 5), having a guide can pay for itself many times over.

Unsecured borrowing

So far, I have explored how compounding can work in your favour. Let's look at how it can work against you. Unsecured borrowing describes any borrowing for which there is no security, no asset for the lender to reclaim in the event the borrower cannot meet their obligations. Common types of unsecured borrowing include credit or store cards, personal loans, car finance agreements, buy now pay later schemes and short-term arrangements like pay day lending. All of these have one thing in common: they are expensive ways of borrowing money.

As the lender has no security against the debt, the risk of that debt not being paid is higher, as will be the cost of recovering and outstanding payments, so the cost of borrowing reflects these two factors. This is why if you have a poor credit rating you can expect to pay more to borrow money, as you are perceived to be a higher risk than someone with an excellent credit rating. Interest rates of around 18% per annum on credit cards are not uncommon and they can be over 50% for those with the lowest credit ratings. A balance of £2,000 at an interest rate of 18% would take more than thirty years to repay in full if you only make the minimum payments of 2% of the balance each month; and that's assuming you do not use your credit card again during those thirty years. Unsecured borrowing can quickly spiral out of control if not managed carefully.

A simple rule with credit cards is always pay off the balance in full each month; that way you do not have to pay any interest at all. In Chapter 2, I mentioned the increased availability of buy now pay later schemes. These schemes encourage poor budgeting and increased spending, leading to opportunity cost and, if not careful, the use of unsecured credit, which can become unsustainable.

Mortgages: think twice about the forty-year option

Mortgage companies tend to use daily compounding when calculating the interest due. I've seen some use this as a marketing strategy, by stating 'we use daily compounding so that your balance is always accurately reflected', rather than 'because it means we can quote an interest rate that looks lower'.

One of the downsides of the boom in property prices over the last thirty years is that it has put home ownership out of reach for many. Mortgage lenders have had to think of new ways to lend to assist people onto the property ladder. With longer life expectancies, meaning later retirement, the traditional twenty-five-year mortgage has now been extended all the way up to forty years. Spreading the cost over a longer term means that the monthly payments are lower, making it appear more affordable. As you might have guessed, this also means that mortgage lenders can now make a much higher return on the same loan.

Over twenty-five years a mortgage of £200,000 at 2.5% interest would cost £897 per month and you would repay a total of £269,170. This same loan over forty years would cost £660 a month, a 'saving' of £237 per month. However, the total amount repaid increases to £316,587. It is always advisable to consider the total cost of borrowing before agreeing to proceed.

7

How To Plan For Financial Independence

So far, we have identified the formulas that need to be understood when it comes to managing your money. Planning for financial independence means leveraging the power of compounding to allow you to accumulate enough wealth to meet your costs for the rest of your life.

The starting point I identified in Chapter 2 is working out what your future lifestyle will cost. After working out how much income you need, you can work out how much money you will need to accumulate by a given age. Using another heuristic, you can calculate how much your total investment portfolio needs to be for you to be financially independent. To keep it simple, multiply the income you need by twenty-five.

As an example, if you need £40,000 a year from age 60, this multiplied by 25 gives you £1,000,000. This is now the target amount of money you need to accumulate. Using the formulas in Chapter 6, you work backwards to work out how much money you need to save each month to accumulate the target amount.

Let's work an example through, assuming you are 30 and need to save £1,000,000 by age 60. I'll use the same 5% growth rate we have been using so far, and the same compounding formula for monthly saving. Last time, we knew the amount that was being saved each month, but didn't know the amount at the end. This time, we know the amount at the end but not the monthly amount. By changing the formula slightly, we can work this out:

$$PMT = \frac{r/n \times FV}{(1 + r/n)^{nt} - 1}$$

where the terms have the same meaning as in Chapter 6, FV means future value, and

$r = 0.05$

$n = 12$ (we are making monthly payments, so twelve payments)

$t = 30$

EXAMPLE

$FV = £1,000,000$

$$PMT = \frac{r/n \times FV}{(1 + r/n)^{nt} - 1}$$

$$= \frac{0.05/12 \times £1m}{(1 + 0.05/12)^{360} - 1}$$

$$= £4,166.67 / (1.00416)^{360} - 1$$

$$= £4,166.67 / 3.46774$$

$$= £1,201.55 \text{ per month}$$

In this example, you would need to save £1,201.55 per month to build up £1,000,000 over a thirty-year period.

This may seem to most people like a huge figure to save each month, and it is. There are a few variables within the calculation that you can play around with to change the monthly amount. One I have already explained is the impact of starting early. Starting at twenty rather than thirty changes the monthly amount to £655.30. Still a lot of money to save, and an impossibility for most 20-year-olds. We can also change the growth rate, from 5% to 7%. Over thirty years, 7% will mean a monthly saving amount of £819.69 and over forty years £380.98. Starting early makes a big difference and so does the rate of return you can achieve.

What about inflation? We saw in Chapter 6 how inflation will erode the future value of your money. To combat this, each year you will need to increase the amount you save by at least the inflation rate over the previous twelve months. There are investment products that will automatically do this for you, otherwise you have to do it personally.

What if you have already started saving and have built up a reasonable fund already? You can work out the total fund value you will need in future the same way, but then you can project what your current investments will be worth if they grow at the rate you used to work out the fund you'll need. Deducting this figure from the total fund value you need will tell you what your future savings need to provide, and then you can work out the monthly savings to provide this using the calculation above.

Passive income

Passive income is income that you receive without having to work for it, and having passive income will help you to become financially independent. You can be classed as financially independent if you have so much money that you could not spend it all before you reach age 100; or you could have enough passive income coming in from assets that it will meet your needs between now and 100 without your having to draw on the capital. In between these positions is a plan for drawing down capital and gradually reducing your income.

Dividends earned from owning shares are a key source of passive income. If you have an investment portfolio generating dividend income that is sufficient for your needs then you are financially independent. Dividends, like the company profits they are based on, typically offer good protection against inflation. Inflation comes from increases in prices, so if these are increasing then that should feed through to higher company turnover, profits and dividend income over time. It doesn't always work out like this, but that is the theory. Companies will face difficulty from time to time, and might not be able to meet their dividend payments sometimes. As I showed in Chapter 5, remaining diversified can reduce this risk, or using an investment fund that is designed to generate income.

Dividends are not the only source of passive income; any income that comes in without you having to work is classed as passive earnings. Property rentals can generate a regular income, as could your own business if it is now able to run without you; royalties for your ideas and writing might be another. I could argue that royalties are not purely passive, since they involve you having to continually promote yourself. The key thing to remember is that passive income comes from assets. If you have to work for it, it is not passive.

Property investing

Property investing is a popular way of becoming financially independent. There are a couple of reasons for this in my experience, the main one being it is tangible: you can touch it. Unless you have researched them, the value of stocks and shares can seem opaque and difficult to grasp. Property is tried and tested and proven to work; but it is not perfect.

If you rely on rental income for the rest of your life then you will need to consider the impact of inflation. With an investment portfolio, you can draw dividends, or sell capital to raise income. Property income is the rents you receive. To protect against inflation, rents would have to be increased each year; but rents are not set by the rate of inflation – they are set by the market. Rents in London have changed little since the end of 2016. Property price growth does not necessarily translate into rent increases, as the market for owners is different from the market for renters.

Another danger is government intervention in the form of rent controls. Several cities around the world have used or currently use rent controls, even though many do not believe they work. If the government sets rents, and not the market, then that means a cap on the return landlords can make. If landlords can get a better return elsewhere, then they may sell their properties and do so. If enough did so, that would lead to a reduction in the number of rental properties available and could mean a fall in house prices in areas where there were more sellers than buyers. However, although it doesn't work, rent control is a tempting move for politicians.

A 2018 research piece by Stanford University on rent controls in San Francisco showed some interesting insights into the impact they have. In 1994 rent controls were expanded, which led to rents falling for tenants to whom the controls applied. The controls didn't apply to newly constructed properties, however, so there were cases of landlords paying up to $30,000 to their tenant as an incentive to leave controlled property, that could then be reconstituted so it didn't fall within the rent control scheme. Between 1994 and 2010 the availability of rent-controlled property fell by 25%. While one generation benefited from lower rents, the following generation had to deal with huge rental costs and a limited supply of properties.[20]

Rent controls have been tried in a number of other cities with varying success, but the important thing for a landlord to remember is never to underestimate the risk that it could happen. Tax changes can also impact your returns, and in the UK several targeted tax changes have left property investors with reduced yields.

---

20 Rebecca Diamond, Tim McQuade & Franklin Qian, 'The effects of rent control expansion on tenants, landlords, and inequality: Evidence from San Francisco', *American Economic Review*, 109/9 (2019).

However, when you take these risks into account property is still a great way to generate income. One of the strengths of investing in properties is that you can borrow money to complete a purchase. Borrowing to fund a purchase reduces the amount of your own capital invested, and as a result increases your yield. Let's look at some examples:

EXAMPLES

In this example, assume you are buying a property worth £200,000 and it rents out for £800 each month. You are buying outright, no borrowing – what is your yield?

£800 × 12 = £9,600

£9,600 / £200,000 = 0.048

0.048 × 100 = 4.8%

Same example, but let's assume you use £100,000 of your own money and borrow £100,000 on an interest-only basis, at a rate of 2%.

£100,000 × 2% = £2,000

£2,000 / 12 = £166.67

(£800 – £166.67) × 12 = £7,599.96

£7,599.96 / £100,000 = 0.076

0.076 × 100 = 7.6%

As you are only using £100,000 of your own money, then you work out the income from the capital you have invested. After deducting the cost of borrowing the yield has increased from 4.8% to 7.6%. In this case, borrowing has enhanced your return.

As a caveat to this example, borrowing is cheap at the time of writing, but it may be more costly in future should interest rates rise.

Borrowing is not the only cost that needs to be taken into account: taxes, void periods (ie when the building is empty) and maintenance costs also need to be calculated and deducted from the gross monthly income to work out a net yield. I won't cover taxes here, so you will need to find out how your country taxes property income.

So far I've ignored increases in the property price, but these would form part of your overall return. If you held an investment property for a period of time and then sold it, your total return would be made up of the income you have received plus any profit that you make on sale, less your costs (including cost of sale). Profits can be subject to tax, which will reduce the overall return that is made. To work out the return from a capital gain, you calculate your profit after deduction of costs and taxes and take into account the number of years you held the property for. This is called a holding period return and here's an example:

EXAMPLE

Property purchased for £150,000 is held for ten years before being sold for £200,000. Ignoring taxes and costs, a £50,000 profit is made.

£50,000 / £150,000 = 33%

$(0.33 + 1)^{1/10} - 1 = 0.0289$

$0.0289 \times 100 = 2.89\%$

The gross profit might be 33%, but as the return came in over ten years, the figure is 2.89% per annum. If you add this to your rental yield you get a total return.

So, using the previous examples, borrowing to buy the property brought in 4.8% per annum, so the total return was 7.49%; and borrowing only half brought in 7.6% per annum, so the total was 10.49%. I've taken a short cut here and used one year's rental yield, where to be accurate you would need to consider the income in each year. Costs and taxes would also need to be taken into account, which will reduce the yield. Taxes in the UK come in the form of income taxes and capital gains taxes, and possibly stamp duty when you bought the property, and these would reduce the yield. Recent tax regime changes in the UK have left some property investors wondering whether the returns are worth the hassle.

Property income does not immediately benefit from compound growth, either. If you recall, over the long term reinvestment of dividends forms a large part of your total return from investment in stocks and shares due to the effects of compounding. Unless you reinvest your property income, it will not benefit from compounding. It is difficult to reinvest property income back into property, as generally you can't buy part of a property each month. However, you could reinvest your income into your investment portfolio and that way you will benefit.

The FIRE movement formula and its limitations

The Financial Independence Retire Early (FIRE) movement uses what it calls a golden formula for financial independence. This involves savings worth twenty-five times your expenses and withdrawing 4% each year from your pot. This rule of thumb was designed for those retiring around age 65 and works reasonably well at that age. However, the effectiveness reduces if you retire below that age and the reason for that is inflation.

Each year your costs increase, so your income would need to increase by at least inflation for you to maintain your lifestyle. Increasing your income means that you are now taking more than 4% from your portfolio and, for that to work, your portfolio needs to have grown enough to support the increase. I will look at this in Chapter 8.

The other effect that inflation will have is on the value of the target that you initially calculate that you need. If you work out that you need £1 million in thirty years' time, by then £1 million is going to be worth much less than it is today. As mentioned in Chapter 6, your strategy to mitigate this is to always increase the amount you save each year by at least the annual rate of inflation.

Inflation will eat away at the portfolio value and it will eat away at the value of the 4% income withdrawn, so what happens? If you plan for financial independence too early, then in all likelihood you will run out of money well before age 100 if you use the 4% rule. For example, were you to use this rule of thumb in a plan to retire at 35, you would be highly likely to run out of money in retirement. For most people saving to retire at 65, however, the formula is a good heuristic to base a financial plan on.

The other limitation of the FIRE movement for me personally is that the ways it prescribes for saving involve sacrificing the potential enjoyment of years of your life through extreme budgeting and cost reduction. This may be highly enjoyable for some, but personally I prefer balance and enjoying myself at all stages of life. I don't think that sacrificing the present for the future is a particularly great plan, on the basis that you never know what the future might bring.

Managing risks

'Everyone has a plan, until they get hit for the first time.'
— Mike Tyson[21]

There is nothing quite like an unexpected emergency that can send a hurricane through your well-laid plans, leaving them in ruins. Never underestimate the risk that during your lifetime there could be a significant event that affects your ability to accumulate wealth, be this loss of a job, business failure, serious illness or the death of someone close to you. All these things can have a catastrophic effect on your savings.

If you stop saving, or have to reduce what you save, then there will be less in the future. If you suffer an emergency that means you have to withdraw money from your fund, you leave a big hole to be filled later. Emergencies usually mean there is not much choice, and if you have to use the money when there is no other option, you will. Two things can help manage the unexpected: cash and insurance.

Cash is absolutely crucial in an emergency, whether to replace an income for a period, pay medical expenses or help repay any outstanding liabilities. A healthy emergency fund held in cash will provide money you can draw on to support you through a problem,

---

21 Reported in 'James Has a Notion Where Blame Belongs', *Sports, Los Angeles Times*, 28 August 1987.

rather than touching your long-term investments. As we saw in the compounding examples in Chapter 6, withdrawing early creates opportunity cost. A sensible cash fund for emergencies will vary for each individual and depend on the risks they are exposed to, but three to six months' expenditure is a minimum. When calculating the amount you need, take not only your essential monthly expenditure into account but also your discretionary spending and, most important, your monthly savings. If you can keep on saving during an emergency, you will feel the benefit later on.

Cash will see you through most short-term emergencies, but what about something more significant or long-term? Insurance. We insure our cars, our homes, our pets, our gadgets, when we travel we take out insurance, but what about ourselves?

If you owned a machine that each month printed out a stack of money, how much would you insure it for against breakdowns? You are that machine.

You can insure your life, your medical bills, your monthly income against short-term sickness or against serious illness. All of these will provide benefits that minimise any impact on your future, or your family's. If you don't have insurance in place, in the event of death the ones you leave behind could struggle financially. Or if you are ill and unable to work, you could struggle to pay the bills, your mortgage and your monthly savings.

You can insure your income with something called income protection. It is designed to pay a set amount of money each month if you are unable to work, and usually it will keep paying until you can return to work. One of the reasons that we don't take insurance is we tell ourselves 'it won't happen to me'. How can you be sure?

Claim statistics from 2018 published by LV (the insurance company) show that, on average, male customers claim on income protection at 46 years old and women at 45. That's younger than you might have expected. The three most common conditions behind claims, according to the Association of British Insurers[22], are:

1. Musculoskeletal – 30%

2. Mental illness – 9%

3. Cancer – 7%

Bad backs are the main type of musculoskeletal injury that causes claimants to cease to be able to work.

Now you've read this chapter you should have a clearer idea on how you might calculate your financial independence goals. Refer to the appendix of this book to find a guidance on building your own financial plan.

---

22 See www.ftadviser.com/protection/2019/06/24/why-income-protection-is-evolving/?page=2

8

Drawdown Strategies

Once you reach the point of having achieved financial independence, you have enough money to theoretically last until you are 100. The next phase is decumulation and starting to spend the income and capital you have saved. It may be a surprise that I mentioned spending capital, but that is the point as money is no good to you at 100. It becomes of less use to you past a certain age. In Chapter 1 I mentioned the thoughts of Marcus Aurelius about how short life is. Consider that there are youthful years where you are restricted in what you can do; towards the end of your life the same occurs. Past a certain age, your health will restrict what you are able to do. Therefore, it is important that you use your money to improve your life and the lives of those around you before you reach that point. To have drawn down successfully would be to spend your last £1 just before you leave this world. However, that isn't easy.

Setting an appropriate strategy

How long we live and when our health will start restricting us, is unknown. Successful drawdown strategies need to manage the risk that you might run out of money. If planned properly you can comfortably withdraw income and capital from the money you accumulated. If the right strategy isn't implemented then the risk of running out of money increases.

In a 2019 report, the World Economic Forum[23] showed that longevity has increased the risk of retirees running out of money. In the UK, the average man will run out of money 9.9 years before their life expectancy and women 12.6 years. The difference between sexes is down to Mrs Average saving less than Mr Average, since she is more likely to take time out of her career to raise children, and the fact that women live longer than men.

Running out of money early can also happen if your investment strategy is not suited to drawdown. When you are accumulating money, volatility can work in

---

23   See www.weforum.org/agenda/2019/06/retirees-will-outlive-their-savings-by-a-decade

your favour. When we looked at pound-cost averaging in Chapter 5, the effect of variance in unit or share prices from month to month averaged out in the long term. Unfortunately, the principle that benefits you when you are saving works against you when you are withdrawing. Too much variance in the month-by-month valuation of your investments can mean that you run out of money far quicker than if you had taken a path of less risk.

EXAMPLE

Let's say you have £100,000 invested and you need to withdraw £4,000 this year to top up your income. The market has just suffered a downturn, meaning your portfolio is now worth 10% less. How much does your investment need to increase by to offset the withdrawal *and* make up the loss?

£100,000 – 10% = £90,000

£90,000 – £4,000 = £86,000

£100,000 – £86,000 = £14,000

£14,000 / £86,000 = 16.28%

While your portfolio may recover from the fall, in order to make up the loss plus the withdrawal it would need to increase by 16.28% before the next withdrawal is taken. This is before inflation is taken into account, which would probably mean a higher withdrawal will be required the next year. This example is crude, as we are only looking at the picture over a year. In reality prices fluctuate daily, and most retirees withdraw a monthly income.

Volatility in investment terms describes the variance in asset prices. The wider the variance between the highs and lows, the greater the volatility. In drawdown, low volatility means a lower risk of running out of money too early. However, low volatility usually means low growth and that means that your portfolio may struggle to fight the effects of inflation. There is a fine balancing act between taking the right level of risk to ensure that you beat inflation, without the risk of running out of money before the end of your life. FIRE's 4% rule of thumb (see Chapter 7) does not take into account the risks that you may be exposed to through your investment portfolio, which is another of its limitations.

If you assumed 5% growth in your portfolio, you might think that taking 4% would leave 1% still invested. However, don't forget that inflation and running costs will erode your investment. If inflation is 2%, that reduces your growth from 5% to 3%; if your running costs are 1.5%, that leaves 1.5% net growth. So, if you withdraw 4% that means that your portfolio would decrease 2.5%, in this example. So over time the value of your portfolio goes down and down, until it runs out. You hope that it won't run out during your lifetime. Hopefully, you can see now that the 4% rule doesn't work that well if you retire early. In my business I use software that carries out for me the complex calculation of drawdown rates against inflation, running costs and future investment returns, as the maths is beyond the scope of this book.

When you are in the accumulation phase, investment portfolios are designed to grow your money. This means a more aggressive investment strategy. For example, if you were investing in shares you would favour companies with high growth prospects. These companies may be less mature, and not pay much in dividends, favouring reinvesting profits to fuel growth. If you wanted income, you would pick a more mature business, with a stable market position and strong record of paying dividends. Mature companies often have little competition and the business they're in presents high barriers to entry, so their share prices are not usually as volatile as a younger company. Portfolios designed to generate income usually favour asset classes that produce regular income, like commercial property or fixed income in the form of government and corporate bonds. Portfolios designed to suit income investors are different from those for growth investors, and so transitioning from accumulating to spending means rethinking your investment strategy.

Many asset managers are already trying to solve the problem of meeting the investment needs of retirees, who will live longer than the generation that came before them. The range of investment approaches for people at this stage of life is ever-increasing.

The traditional approach used to be using your retirement fund to buy an annuity, an income that is usually guaranteed to be paid for your whole life. These fell out of favour in the financial crisis as interest rates fell to record lows, so the price rose. Many investors preferred to take the risk of remaining invested. Remaining in control of your retirement fund offers you control over how much you withdraw, allowing for higher spending while you are young and lower spending when you are older – with all the risks that entails.

You can buy an annuity at any time, so once health starts declining and (perhaps) spending reduces, annuities may help solve the problem of running out of money in later life.

I mentioned earlier that paying for care in later life can become a reality for many. The cost of care can ravage savings. A Bupa study from 2011 indicated that the average stay in a care home is 801 days.[24] In 2019, the average cost for residential care was £33,852, which increased to £47,320 per year if nursing care was required.[25] Using these figures, on average, it could cost £74,288.91 for end-of-life residential care or £103,844.71 for nursing care, although there is significant variation depending on the length of stay required.

In the UK, the state currently only pays if your savings are below certain thresholds. If you have your own savings, then your care costs are self-funded.

---

24 See https://eprints.lse.ac.uk/33895/1/dp2769.pdf
25 See www.payingforcare.org/how-much-does-care-cost

Philanthropy

Research at the University of Toronto by Stéphane Côté, Julian House and Robb Willer found that higher-income individuals are less generous than lower-income individuals. Research by Comparethemarket.com on generosity showed that, while the average person donates around 2.23% of their lifetime earnings to charity, 72% of the world's fifty richest people donate less than this. There are some exceptions, Bill Gates and Warren Buffett are two of the most generous billionaires, having given away 55% and 45% of their wealth already.

When we give money, a few things happen in our brains which neuroscience dubs the 'helper's high'. When we give and help others, our brains release a cocktail of oxytocin, serotonin and dopamine. Oxytocin is the chemical that gets released when we hug people, that warm fuzzy feeling that makes us feel good. The effect of these hormones on us increases our mood and enables us to better cope with stress.

The common way that people give is through a registered charity, and while that is a perfectly legitimate way of giving, you are unable to see the impact it has. A Charities Aid Foundation report in 2019 found that 50% of women view charities as trustworthy versus 47% of men, and 18% and 23% respectively view charities as untrustworthy. Some charities have grown into huge organisations now, and while many do amazing work these trust levels could be due to a perception of how much of your donation may disappear in costs. The Charity Commission website allows you to check how much UK charities spend on charitable activities, and on their running costs.

A way to increase the benefit that comes from gifting is to be directly involved, rather than indirectly. Your time is one of the most valuable commodities you can give, as it is a thing that you have a finite amount of. Combining gifts of money with direct involvement will boost the return you get from any giving you choose to do. What big causes align with your purpose, which you could become involved in? If you can find a cause that aligns with your values and passion, then you will freely give your time.

Inheritance tax and giving while alive

If your financial planning has gone exceptionally well, you may find yourself in a position where you have more money than you can get through during the rest of your life. When they start to draw down their savings, some people may be in this position and not know it. If you don't know that you have more money than you will need for yourself, then you may well retain money through fear of running out. If you knew that based on conservative assumptions you would never run out, new options open up. You could increase your lifestyle spending, you could engage in philanthropy, or you could use your money to help younger generations of your family while you are alive.

In the UK, the tax regime states that on death your assets are valued and, above a certain level, the balance is subject to inheritance tax, currently at 40%. Now it isn't you that pays it, it is the people named in your will that stand to lose out to the tax office. Let's say you are worth £3m on death and have three children; after allowances and tax, each child would receive £686,666. The tax office would receive £940,000, far exceeding the amount left to each of your offspring.

While you won't be alive to pay this tax, there is a lost opportunity – you could have given the money away and seen the impact that it has while you were alive. This would reward you in the same way that philanthropy does, but differently, as you see the impact that it has on younger generations of your family.

In my experience of advising people at this stage of life, balance is key. Giving too much help might hinder your children from finding their own path in life, make them dependent upon handouts, mean that they don't take their own lives seriously. This can be managed by creating rules about how and when you may help. I believe that the best investment you can ever make is in your own education. I have continuously studied over my career, learning new skills and qualifications. This is a never-ending process for me.

My father retired this year (2020), having worked for the same company since before I was born. For my generation, that is becoming more rare and rarer still for the generation below me. I was made redundant in 2011, then I joined a new company only to be made redundant six months later. Luckily, I secured another job within the same company, which a year later ended up being restructured. Eventually I got fed up and left to set up my own business. The coronavirus crisis means that for many another round of redundancies is on the horizon, meaning people my age will have been through two major economic crises before the age of 40, combined with lower average earnings than recent generations and higher cost of housing relative to income.

The 'job for life' is far less common now and, for the next fifty years, the most important skill is probably going to be ability to adapt and learn new skills. A good use of capital, when it comes to gifting, would be to help fund the cost of qualifications or financial support if study is full-time. Education will help younger members of your family develop themselves, their commitment to life-long learning and their outlook on life.

Children's savings

During your lifetime, if you take the first twenty-two years for education and on average thirty-five years at the end for drawdown, you have forty-three years over which to make compounding work for you. If you want to extend that further, save for your children's future.

Starting saving for children from their birth extends those forty-three years to sixty-five years. As the exponential effect of compounding really takes hold after thirty years, sixty-five years has huge potential to change your child's life. If we use the rule of 72, a 7% return will double roughly every ten years. That means an investment made for a child at birth and left until drawdown at 65, would double six times. To put that in perspective, £5,000 might grow to £320,000.

This is the way to view children's savings, rather than 'use it for a car at 18'. In Chapter 6 I talked about the paradox that, to leverage compounding, you must start early, at the same time as being stuck with low earnings, potentially student debt, pressure to find a place in society and the problem of saving enough for a house deposit. By helping your children make an early start on their journey to financial independence, you could change their lives.

Going back to an earlier example, let's say you start a savings account for your child, and pay for the first twenty years. As your child grows older, you start educating them about the importance of saving monthly, and what you have done for them so far. You let them know that one day you will hand over to them and it will be their job to keep the payments going. To save

£1m by the time they reach 60, the two of you would need to save £219.75 per month.

Money habits are learned by age 7, so if you take this approach you have a golden opportunity to bring your child up with the right attitudes towards financial independence. I learned the hard way, and didn't understand debt, budgeting or compounding until I trained as a financial adviser. I remember having many conversations with friends about what I was learning, and realising that it was not just me that was wholly uneducated about the basics of money. This has not changed, as even now I meet young people who are amazed by the simplicity of some of the ideas and concepts in this book. They always say the same thing: 'Why didn't I get taught this in school?'

9

Selling Your Business

What is your business worth?

If someone walked into your office and put a cheque on the table, how do you know whether you should take it?

In Chapter 2 I mentioned that a number of business owners become obsessed with the idea that selling their business will be their retirement plan. The problem is, most have never taken the time to work out how much they would need to sell their business for in order to be financially independent and have enough money for the rest of their life.

Over the years I've heard many reasons why the business is guaranteed to find a buyer, why this can't go wrong or how a better return on capital can be made within the business than outside. All of these arguments mean the same thing, that if you believe that your business is your retirement plan, you are entirely dependent upon it. There is no plan B. If there is no plan B, then a problem with your business will mean that you will not have enough money to fund your lifestyle, and might not even be able to sell it.

Anything can happen in business: your biggest clients could leave, another company could create a product that replaces your entire business sector, a recession could hit at the time you want to sell or, more often than not, no one wants to buy, your business is not ready for sale.

How can you be sure that when you want to sell, you receive enough money to meet the costs of your lifestyle for the rest of your life?

The amount you need and the date you need it by

If you know how much money you need to be financially independent at a given age, then you are in a powerful position if an offer is made for your business. You know whether you should accept it or not. Imagine if someone offered you twice as much as you needed and you were not looking to sell at that point: what would you do?

For entrepreneurs, the process of working out how much you need to become financially independent needs to be followed. You should aim to build up capital to be financially independent of the business, and now no longer reliant upon a sale. If you achieve this a couple of things happen. Firstly, the risk has gone and you don't have to worry about an uncertain future any more. Secondly, if you don't need to sell the business then you can structure it so that you only do the work that you find most enjoyable and that gives you the greatest sense of purpose.

A plan to get from A to B

If your plan still involves the sale of your business, in part or entirely, then you can think ahead and make sure your business is worth what you need it to be, come the time you sell. If your business is not currently worth what it needs to be, then you have discovered where you need to get to.

Entrepreneurs are creative and given a problem, with the right approach they can come up with solutions. Now, if you had a value that you knew your business needed to be worth by a given date in the future, ask yourself – what would my business need to look like to be worth that? You might pause for a minute, but quickly you will start coming up with answers. You might work out what your turnover would need to be, what your organisational structure would look like, what key people would need to be in the business, your costs, the clients you work with and so on and so on.

Very quickly, you build a plan of what your future business looks like. You can now think about how you get from where you are now to where you want to be, by working backwards to today and discovering the smallest steps that can be taken now.

The business that runs without you

For how long could you go on holiday, with no contact with your office, before your turnover was affected? One week, one month, six months, twelve months? If part of your financial future depends upon the sale of your business, then you need to start getting it ready for sale now, even if you plan to sell in ten or twenty years' time. Steven Covey said in *The 7 Habits of Highly Successful People* 'start with the end in mind'. By thinking ahead about what your business needs to look like to attract the value you want, you can also plan to remove yourself from the day-to-day operation of the company.

There are two other benefits of extracting yourself from the everyday running of your business: it's more attractive for a buyer if the business has a team of people who can run it without the owner, and it means that you are no longer involved in work that you feel you have to do rather than want to do. In *The E-Myth* Michael Gerber describes the scenario that most small business owners find themselves in. When you start the company, you are excited about building up a company and then having financial freedom and loads of time. The reality is, quickly you realise that it doesn't happen that way. You work evenings, you work weekends, you go on holiday and you check your emails and answer the phone.

Comes with an operating manual

Whoever buys your company needs to be able to run it without you. Your business is worth more if it comes with an operating manual, and by that I mean that your procedures and processes are written down. There is no good in an owner with all the knowledge walking out. I went through an exercise a couple of years ago starting to record everything that we did within the company, so that we could review and improve what we do. The by-product of that is that each job role and process is written down in a process manual that can be taught to new joiners and is also available if someone were to come and buy the business.

Recurring revenues and exits

If your business has passive income, then it is far more attractive to a buyer. Passive income within a business removes some of the risk of the business suddenly seeing a drop in turnover because the owner has left. In most small businesses, the owner is the face of the business, the one who all the clients know, and a potential buyer will wonder how long they would continue to do business with your company if you left it.

Without recurring revenues, the purchase is riskier for the buyer than for the seller. At least with recurrent revenues, the buyer has an income stream that they could use to help finance the purchase; without that, their investment needs to be paid back through the future revenues of the business. The owner leaving presents too big a risk for most purchasers, and consequently the deal structure on exit may involve no money upfront at all. A lot of small business owners are unprepared for this reality, only coming to terms with it after a few years trying to sell and finding no one wants to part with their cash.

Eventually the owner comes to the conclusion that they either liquidate and get paid nothing, or accept an offer that involves no money upfront. No money upfront doesn't mean no money at all, it means that the purchase may be paid for via an earn-out over a few years: a series of staged payments out of profits of the business. This mitigates some of the risk for the buyer, as the owner is now engaged and has an interest in the continuing success of the company. The payment for the business could be deferred, and conditional on the company meeting certain criteria. If the business fails to achieve the contractual obligations (targets, changes in approach or model, R&D, whatever), the payment could be reduced or not paid at all. Assets within the business, such as plant and machinery or property, could be sold to pay the exiting owner. Of course, a combination of these structures could be put together to fund the owner's exit. The point is, there are several ways that a business can be sold where no money changes hands on exit day.

There is nothing wrong with exiting using these structures, as they provide a perfectly legitimate route to exit for many business owners. If you plan to exit and receive a lump sum for your business, then your business needs to be in shape for that to happen. It needs to be attractive and a low-risk purchase for your buyer. That requires planning.

Business aligned to personal goals

I believe that business owners have a unique perspective on financial independence. The act of starting your own business puts your success firmly in your own hands, rather than that of an organisation you work for. Most entrepreneurs started off employed and at some stage decided it wasn't for them. Financial independence should be the goal of every entrepreneur, and most importantly, achievable without relying on the sale of the business.

Entrepreneurs can be some of the worst at putting off financial planning, and as we saw in Chapter 6, that can be detrimental. The reason entrepreneurs are the worst is that every day can be a work day, and there are always more important problems to deal with. My accountant likes to remind me of the difference between time in the business and time working on the business. The same applies to time working in the business and time working on your life.

A business aligned to the achievement of your long-term financial goals and purpose will keep you happy and engaged. Make your business your reason to wake up in the morning, your *ikigai* (see Chapter 1). Of course, when you are financially independent outside your business, you are less reliant upon a cash sale. This means you can consider other exit structures for your business that work for both you and your buyer. They could even involve you staying in the company, doing work that you love doing.

10

Taking Advice

George S. Clason's wise advice in *The Richest Man in Babylon* (1926) is as pertinent now as it was nearly a century ago. His words illustrate the imperative of taking financial advice from a trusted and experienced professional:

'Why trust the knowledge of a brickmaker about jewels? Would you go to the breadmaker to inquire about the stars?

No, by my tunic, you would go to the astronomer, if you had power to think. And next time if you would have advice about jewels, go to the jewel merchant. If you would know the truth about sheep, go to the herdsman.

Advice is one thing that is freely given away, but watch that you take only what is worth having. He who takes advice about his savings from one who is inexperienced in such matters, shall pay with his savings for proving the falsity of their opinions.'

Advice is worth paying for. You can go and join a gym, pay the membership fee, but you have to do the work. You have to turn up, you have to come up with your own exercise routine, your own diet plan, clearly define your fitness goals, motivate yourself, stay motivated! Or you can pay for a fitness coach who will help you define your goals, design your plan, motivate you, challenge you and through them you achieve more, far faster than had you been left to do it yourself.

Taking advice not only gives you shortcuts and gets you taking actions, it also saves you a lot of time having to learn how to do it yourself. People who manage their own money, the do-it-yourself managers, will hopefully have learned a lot in this book that can help them manage their money better. The delegators may have had their decision to take advice confirmed, having seen the amount of work that is required.

For business owners, there is an additional adviser that can be brought in to help – the accountant. An accountant who really understands financial planning and the benefits it brings can play an important role for a business owner. The accountant can help the business owner build business plans that create more income and sales, find cost savings, save tax, advise how to get the profits out the business, assist with due diligence for a sale, work out a target exit value and even help with deal structures on exit. Combined with a financial planner who works the way set out in this book, an entrepreneur has a strong team set to help them succeed.

Of course, as the quote above shows, it pays to listen to the right people. Do your homework, question people's motives and avoid listening to the opinions of the inexperienced.

My approach

I started working as a financial adviser for a high street bank in 2008, having been accepted into their training academy. I spent six months attending workshops and courses, plus time observing experienced financial advisers – some who had been doing the job for over thirty years. I had completed the required qualifications, the Certificate for Financial Advisers, in my previous role where I investigated complaints made against the advice given by the bank. I remember having a conversation with a colleague who joined the bank in the 1980s, who told me the interview was one question: 'Do you want the job?'

Before 1988 no minimum qualifications were required at all; often the 'advisers' knew 1% more than the client. Then in 1988 new regulations came in and financial advisers had to sit Financial Planning Certificates 1, 2 and 3. Today these would be equivalent to GCSE level (O-Levels if you did those). Basically, there was not a huge amount to learn for the qualification.

Financial Planning Certificates 1, 2 and 3 were at some point replaced by the Certificate for Financial Advisers, or CeFA. A few exam bodies in the UK award these qualifications. This was the minimum level of qualification required, right up until 2012 – a surprising twenty-four years later! No wonder that in that time we saw mis-selling of pensions in the 1980s and 1990s, of pension mortgages and endowment assurances... Trust in financial advisers was destroyed in those years and remains low to this day. Financial advisers are often mistrusted because people perceive that they will only be recommended products that benefit the adviser. Having started my career investigating mis-sold financial products, this perception is not unjustified.

In 2012, the UK regulator stated that approved advisers were required to increase their knowledge and sit further professional qualifications. The bar was raised to a Qualifications and Credit Framework (QCF) Level 4 Diploma, which is about the equivalent of A-Levels, so still not even the equivalent of a degree. This is the minimum qualification required in the UK to become a regulated financial adviser, and even today about 75% hold the minimum qualification required. This is despite the fact that there are several routes to study for higher-level qualifications, the highest award being Chartered status in one of several professional bodies.

The Chartered Wealth Manager qualification I hold sits at QCF Level 7, the same level as a Masters degree. The only excuse I can see for UK advisers not holding Chartered status is simply that they are not committed to their own development or professionalism. A phrase I often use to explain my love of learning is 'you don't know what you don't know'. I find reading and learning a humbling experience, as it makes you realise how much more there is to learn, and it excites me to do so. I've met advisers over the years who don't see the point of additional qualifications, seeing their 'experience' as proof that they know it all already, and couldn't possibly learn anything new. This arrogance scares me, and it should scare you too. In my definition, experience is gained through applying learning in a practical way. You cannot gain experience through practice alone; it must be combined with study. There are many things I have learned, which I would never have understood without study – or, most importantly, understood their true relevance. The opposite is true too; you cannot gain experience through study alone.

When I started working as a financial adviser the salary was low and the bonuses were high. I was trained in the bank's sales process, designed to sell products to the customers in the branches. We had monthly team meetings, which were usually hosted by the business development arm of an external provider. We were wined and dined for one purpose only, so that we would be encouraged to sell their products.

Over the years I worked in banking I became despondent and always felt that there was a better way of doing the job. Eventually I left to set up my own business, and as that grew I still had this feeling there was something missing. I have been interested in personal development from my early 20s, since reading my first Tony Robbins book. I've always believed in the power of your own mind and that we have the ability to do great things, once we focus. Money plays such an important role in our lives and crisscrosses our plans for life. The penny-drop moment came when I started working with a business coach, who encouraged me to start thinking about my purpose outside work, what I did with my time and who I spent it with. We talked about financial independence being the keystone that allows you to live a great life, and suddenly I realised that my job was to educate my clients about this.

When you work with a coach/life coach to help you make plans for the future, they can assist you in thinking big, breaking through limiting beliefs and breaking down a scary goal into small, achievable objectives. The one thing they can't do, though, is show you how your money fits in. A financial planner trained in coaching is a powerful ally, as not only can they help you plan and dream, they can make the seemingly unachievable achievable.

Imagine being stuck, wondering what you should do with your career. A coach can help you explore your purpose, what you excel at naturally, what you love doing, but what they can't tell you is how much money you need to earn. Your financial planner can. As explained in this book, you can calculate how much money you need to become financially independent and work back to how much you need to save today. If you are not earning enough to save the target amount, you know what you need to do – earn more. Through the financial planning process you can find out how much you need to earn. If you know how much you need to earn, it's far easier to start thinking what steps you need to take to do that in your own career.

Let's say you earn £50,000 today and you need to increase that to £80,000. Within your current job, think what role would pay that: perhaps your manager's job, or their boss's job. Look at that role and ask yourself 'what skills does that person have that I don't?' Do you need to go and invest in a management course, read leadership books, work on your CV? There are many actions you could take when you know what the goal is.

For business owners, you set your own earnings and if you want to be paid more, you have to find a way of growing the business to do that. When you know your target earnings, you can ask yourself, 'What would my business need to look like to pay me £X per year?'

Today, the way I work is completely different from the way that I was first trained. Once the penny had dropped about what my purpose was, I invested further in my own development and studied neuro-linguistic programming, gaining a practitioner certificate. I also studied for a QCF Level 4 Executive Coaching Diploma. Today, the work that I do truly puts my client and their life first. Only once I have helped them understand the role that money plays in their life and their future, do I start the process of building a financial plan. The financial plan uses the concepts in this book to work out how much is needed to become financially independent, to live a great life. The last piece of work required is financial advice, providing recommendations on financial products and investment strategies suitable to support the plan.

There is a growing community globally of financial planners who believe what I believe. This community helps each other with training and development about what the job really amounts to. Sadly, this community is small. The vast majority of financial advisers are there to sell you a product, and either have no real understanding of the concepts in this book, or don't care.

These advisers will not tell you how much you need to become financially independent, they won't tell you how much you need to save, they won't tell you what risks you are exposed to, they won't protect you from bad decisions and the whole time you will wonder whether their fees are worth it – they are not.

Why is this so important? If you don't know what you need to do to become financially independent, you run the risk of not saving enough and running out of money. You could die with too much money, having not spent it for fear of running out and regret all the things you didn't get to do. You could end up working longer than you need to, when actually you could have retired early. You could have spent years working in a job you didn't enjoy because you felt you needed the money. Or you could have spent more, on great experiences with people you love, with the confidence that you were able to do so. You might make emotional decisions with your investments, impacting your long-term returns, or spend your money unwisely, not having been reminded of its time value (see Chapter 6). Sadly, many financial advisers don't understand this, and their businesses are based around selling financial products. In doing so, the important stuff never gets done. I believe that you can't even begin to discuss financial products without having a plan in place first. It is like your doctor writing out a prescription before they have diagnosed you.

This point is completely missed by the UK media, too. Several articles over the years have drawn attention to the practices of certain firms or individuals. The focus is always on the negative, never the positive. So the yarn that all financial advisers are untrustworthy continues to be spun, while the good that great financial planners do goes unheard of. It is absolutely right that companies and individuals should be called out for poor practices, but at the same time an alternative should be offered. Media tend to sell doom and gloom, and we tend to buy it. Many people fly the flag for financial planning done properly, but unfortunately they will never make headlines. Remember, experience is the application of learning to practice. There are several journalists providing helpful money management hints and tips, which will undoubtedly be useful to many. Still, a large portion of the journalism focuses on financial products, their cost and performance; hardly any mentions the importance of a financial plan. All this noise drowns out the real benefits of financial planning, and unfortunately will put many people off engaging the services of a financial planner. (See the appendix on the next few pages for ideas on how to approach and create your own financial plan.)

Paying for advice is worth it if you can find someone who will help you organise your thoughts about money, challenge you to expand your thinking, work with you to build your plan for financial independence, help you work out what you need to earn in your career, protect you from making emotional decisions and provide suitable technical advice about financial products when needed. Most importantly, they help you understand the role that your money needs to play for you to live a wonderful and purposeful life. My aim with this book has been to help you improve your approach regardless of whether you are a do-it-yourselfer or a delegator.

Responsible consumption

The principle of compounding applies to all sorts of different things, among them population growth. It took 127 years for the global population to grow from 1 billion to 2 billion and since 1960 it has grown by 1 billion every 13 years. If that trend continues, then the current population – 7.8 billion (2020) – will double to 15 billion by 2120. You might think, 'Well, I won't be alive then', but your children could be, and maybe their children.

If I live to be 100, the global population will likely increase to 12 billion, a huge increase on what it is today. There is already pressure on resources globally, and as the population grows that will continue. Even if the population stopped growing today, more and more people would become increasingly economically active. As emerging countries develop, a greater portion of the population start receiving higher incomes and with that comes higher consumption.

Having sailed in many seas I have seen the impact that plastic has on the oceans, first-hand. I have been on secluded beaches out of reach from anywhere but the sea and seen them filled with plastic. Writing this book, I realised that with financial independence comes a responsibility to use money not only for your own happiness, but for the health of the planet. We know that stuff doesn't make us happy, so think twice about how you spend and invest your money.

If you can buy second-hand, buy second-hand. A car is a car, a table is a table. I love second-hand furniture shops, the pieces have far more character and each bump and scratch has a story. Throwaway fashion has far more damaging impact on the planet than people realise. It takes 20,000 litres of water to produce 1 kilogram of cotton. The Aral Sea in Asia has been almost drained by water extraction to grow cotton. When you combine this with the fertilisers and pesticides needed to raise the plant, and the chemicals needed to process and dye it, all of which find themselves back in waterways, the effects are devastating. Often clothing ends up in landfill rather than being recycled; often it is worn once only.

It's not just the things we buy but also the things we do that count. I've mentioned prioritising experiences over stuff a number of times in this book, but even then we have a responsibility to consume appropriately. My wife and I have often visited places filled with tourists and joked, 'Wouldn't it be great if all the people weren't here?' Many tourist hotspots have been overrun and the impact from travel there and back, waste left behind and damage to the landscape is unsustainable. I've realised that I have been part of the problem, having visited many of these hotspots over the years. So while experiences will bring you much more joy than buying things, I'd urge you to think about the impact they have.

APPENDIX

The Financial Plan

Now we have covered the principles you need to consider for your financial independence, it is important to formulate your own financial plan.

Why? Well, capturing this into a document makes it real. It holds you to account. It is easy in the 'busy-ness' of life to procrastinate over financial planning but as we have discussed, time can fly and it can be easy to lose sight of your goals and purpose.

This task takes time and thought; so create the space to develop something which is aspirational but also realistic, accurate and reasonable. Using a template like this one here will help you to collect your thoughts into one simple document and remind you what you need to consider under each heading.

The plan outlines a series of headings; you should aim to have a strategy for each. Use the middle column to reflect on each area and what it means to you; I have included some key questions you should answer in each column. The final column gives you space to record your headline financial goals. I have included some tips and reminders of sections in the book you can review to ensure you are considering all aspects and are arriving at an accurate goal.

Before you begin, you may also find it helpful to carry out the Financial Health Check Scorecard which can be found on my website at https://woodfallwealth. scoreapp.com. This may help you to identify gaps in your financial plan and allow you to formulate strategies for tackling them.

	What does this mean to me?	My financial goal is:
Purpose	What is your purpose? What gets you out of bed in the morning?	Review the *ikigai* content in Chapter 1. Take time to review your purpose and capture it in a few short sentences.
	What are your goals for your business?	
	What are your goals for your personal life?	

	What does this mean to me?	*My financial goal is:*
Define financial independence	What does it look like to you? Think about a point in your life you would like to attain independence. What risks or threats could prevent you from attaining independence? How could you mitigate these risks?	Write a short summary of your goals for financial independence and when you will achieve them. Review Chapter 2 on what financial independence means.
Expenditure	What do you regularly spend each month? What could change in your expenditure? Do you envisage it going up, or down?	Do you plan a realistic expenditure budget and do you review it regularly? Make time to do so every quarter. Record your expenditure here. See Chapter 4 about the benefits of budgeting.

	What does this mean to me?	My financial goal is:
Work out how much you need to save, including lump-sum expenses	How much can you save each month? Where will you save it? Remind yourself regularly what you are saving for, so that you can motivate yourself to spend less and save more. Make a note of it here.	Using the guidance about saving from Chapter 4, set a realistic regular savings budget. Consider how much of your income you could divert into savings each month. Then set your savings goal.
Decide whether you will select your own investments or take advice	What investment options do you have? What time and expertise do you have to research your own investment choices? Who would you trust to advise you? Have you researched their track record?	Be honest with yourself about your comfort zone – do you have the confidence in your own expertise? Consider the time you have available to research investment choices and to make well-thought-through decisions. Research your advisers to ensure you trust their advice. Look for professional accreditation and impartiality. Record here if you decide to do this yourself and if not, which financial advisers you will use. See Chapter 10 for more.

	What does this mean to me?	*My financial goal is:*
Don't forget inflation and costs	When putting together your financial plan, consider how inflation can affect your forecasting. Do your savings deposits increase to take into account inflation?	See Chapter 6 for some important pointers to consider when factoring inflation into your plan.
Managing risks	Have you got an emergency fund of at least three months' expenses? Have you considered how long you could last without an income?	Identify the risks that you may be exposed to and note them here. Review your exposure across your portfolio. Make changes to spread your risk if you feel over-exposed. Chapter 5 on Behavioural Finance provides an overview of perception of risk and behaviour.

	What does this mean to me?	*My financial goal is:*
Drawdown strategy	Only relevant at drawdown. If you are not in drawdown yet, skip this step. Consider how your investment strategy needs to change. Review your expenditure in the early and later part of retirement.	Revisit your expenditure against your plan. Underestimating expenses can mean you risk exhausting your funds in retirement. Take a look at Chapter 8 for more information.
Helping younger generations	Skip this step if you don't feel it is relevant to your circumstances. Do you understand the challenges that younger members of your family may face? Have you had a conversation with younger members of your family about wealth?	Record here any provision you will make for future generations if any. See Chapter 8 for help on this topic.

	What does this mean to me?	My financial goal is:
Accountability and action	How are you going to hold yourself accountable?	The key to getting ahead is getting started. Action is the main tool to make your plan real.
	Have you got anyone else involved in the plan, and can you hold each other accountable?	List the milestones dates when you will review the plan to ensure you remain accountable.
Review	How often will you review your plans? (I suggest every six months.)	Any time there is a material change in your circumstances, revisit your plan.
	What will you do to celebrate when you have achieved financial independence?	Over time your priorities will change, so keep updating your plan as you go. Use this section to record when you reviewed the plan, and what you changed.

Now you have a working financial plan, don't lock it into a drawer and forget about it! This should be a living document that you refer to regularly. Put it somewhere visible or calendarise an opportunity every six months to check it.

Ensure you are on track; if you deviate due to unexpected events take time to revise it. Let your plan be your financial satnav, guiding you to your destination. Treat it as your passport to financial independence. Imagine your future self, enjoying your favourite past-time (for me, it would be sailing on a yacht somewhere breath-taking).

References

Brown, H. Jackson, Jr, *P.S. I Love You* (Nashville, TN: Thomas Nelson, Inc., 2000 [1990])

Charities Aid Foundation, *CAF UK Giving 2019*, www.cafonline.org/about-us/publications/2019-publications/uk-giving-2019, accessed 21 July 2020

Charles Schwab Corporation, *2019 Annual Report*, https://content.schwab.com/web/retail/public/about-schwab/schwab_annual_report_2019.pdf, accessed 17 July 2020

Clason, George S., *The Richest Man in Babylon* (New York: Penguin/Random House, 1989 [1926])

Clear, James, *Atomic Habits* (self-published, 2018), https://jamesclear.com/atomic-habits, accessed 17 July 2020

Comparethemarket.com, 'Philanthropic billionaires', www.comparethemarket.com/business-insurance/content/philanthropic-billionaires, accessed 21 July 2020

Côté, Stéphane, Julian House & Robb Willer, 'High economic inequality leads higher-income individuals to be less generous', *Proceedings of the National Academy of Sciences of the USA*, 112/52 (2015), www.pnas.org/content/112/52/15838, accessed 21 July 2020

Covey, Stephen R., *The 7 Habits of Highly Effective People: Powerful lessons in personal change* (New York: Free Press, 2004 [1989])

Csikszentmihalyi, Mihaly, *Flow: the psychology of optimal experience* (New York: Harper & Row, 1990)

Diamond, Rebecca, Tim McQuade & Franklin Qian, 'The effects of rent control expansion on tenants, landlords, and inequality: Evidence from San Francisco', *American Economic Review*, 109/9 (2019), www.gsb.stanford.edu/faculty-research/publications/effects-rent-control-expansion-tenants-landlords-inequality-evidence, accessed 20 July 2020

Expedia and the Center for Generational Kinetics, 'Generations on the Move', 2018, https://viewfinder.

expedia.com/wp-content/uploads/2018/01/
Expedia-Generations-on-the-Move.pdf, accessed 16
July 2020

Garcia, Hector and Francesc Miralles, trans. Heather
Cleary, *Ikigai: The Japanese Secret to a Long and Happy
Life* (Harmondsworth: Penguin, 2017)

Gerber, Michael E., *The E-Myth: Why most businesses
don't work and what to do about it* (self-published, 1986)

Graham, Benjamin, *The Intelligent Investor* (New York:
Harper Business, 2006 [1949])

Jung, Carl, *Modern Man in Search of a Soul* (London:
Routledge Classics, 2001 [1931])

Kahneman, Daniel, 'Of 2 minds: How fast and slow
thinking shape perception and choice', *Scientific
American*, 15 June 2012, www.scientificamerican.
com/article/kahneman-excerpt-thinking-fast-and-
slow, accessed 17 July 2020

Kahneman, Daniel and Angus Deaton, 'High
income improves evaluation of life but not
emotional well-being', *Proceedings of the National
Academy of Sciences of the USA*, 107/38 (2010), www.
pnas.org/content/107/38/16489.short?utm_
content=buffere343c&utm_medium=social&utm_
source=facebook.com&utm_campaign=buffer,
accessed 17 July 2020

Kurzweil, Ray, *How to Create a Mind: The secret of human thought revealed* (Harmondsworth: Penguin, 2013)

Liverpool Victoria Financial Services Ltd, 'Claims', www.lv.com/adviser/claims/claims-performance, accessed 20 July 2020

Marcus Aurelius, *Meditations*, ed. and trans. Maxwell Staniforth (Harmondsworth: Penguin Classics, 1964)

Newman, Cathy, 'How to live to a ripe old age', *National Geographic*, 29 December 2012, www. nationalgeographic.com/news/2012/12/121227-dan-buettner-health-longevity-100-centenarians-science-blue-zones, accessed 15 July 2020

O'Shea, Gary and Maloney, Alison, 'No regrets', *The Sun*, 11 February 2019, www.thesun.co.uk/ news/8402541/how-national-lottery-lout-michael-carroll-blew-9-7m-pounds, accessed 16 July 2020

Office for National Statistics, 'Life Expectancy Calculator', 2019, www.ons.gov.uk/ peoplepopulationandcommunity/healthandsocialcare/ healthandlifeexpectancies/articles/ lifeexpectancycalculator/2019-06-07, accessed 16 July 2020

Rohwedder, Susann and Willis, Robert J., 'Mental retirement', *Journal of Economic Perspectives*, 24/1 (2010)

Statman, Meir, *What Investors Really Want: Discover what drives investor behavior and make smarter financial decisions* (self-published, 2010), https://whatinvestor-swant.wordpress.com/meirs-book-what-investors-really-want, accessed 17 July 2020

Tegmark, Max, *Life 3.0: Being human in the age of artificial intelligence* (Harmondsworth: Penguin, 2018)

Thaler, Richard, 'Mental accounting matters', *Journal of Behavioral Decision Making*, 12 (1999)

Waldinger, Robert, 'What makes a good life? Lessons from the longest study on happiness', www.ted.com/talks/robert_waldinger_what_makes_a_good_life_lessons_from_the_longest_study_on_happiness?language=en#t-16083, accessed 17 July 2020

Whitebread, David and Bingham, Sue, 'Habit Formation and Learning in Young Children', Money Advice Service, 2013, www.moneyadviceservice.org.uk/en/corporate/habit-formation-and-learning-in-young-children, accessed 16 July 2020

Winn, Marc, 'What is your Ikigai?', The View Inside Me blog, 2014, https://theviewinside.me/what-is-your-ikigai

Yorkshire Building Society, 'Exploring the UK's Attitude to Saving Money', 2019, www.ybs.co.uk/media-centre/savings-research/index.html, accessed 16 July 2020

Acknowledgements

I'd like to thank all the clients that have worked with me with over the years. It has been my experience of working with and helping you plan your finances and lives that has led me to writing this book.

I would also like to thank the team at Rethink Press for making this a reality. Writing a book is a daunting task and initially I had no idea how I would go about it. The process and coaching workshop have been extremely helpful.

My team at Woodfall Wealth deserve thanks for their input and inspiration in putting this book together.

Thank you to John Gates, Michael Necati, Teresa McEwan and Molly Pile.

Finally, thanks go to my wife Nicki, who has supported me wonderfully in this and all my endeavours.

The Author

James started his career in financial services in 2004, working for a high street bank. After progressing through the business, he began working as a financial planner in 2008. In 2014, James launched his first company that continues to grow each year. James is a Chartered Fellow of the Chartered Institute for Securities and Investment, having attained their Chartered Wealth Manager qualification, recognised as the gold standard of the profession in the UK.

James has always had a keen interest in psychology and personal development. Through working with his clients, he came to realise that financial planning is the perfect context in which to have a personal development discussion. Money plays such an integral role in all our lives – we work for it, we spend it and we save it for the future. James believes that financial planning should be a fun activity that allows us to create bigger futures and put in place the actions that can make it real.

James qualified as an executive coach in 2020 and is also a certified NLP practitioner, qualifications that ensure his clients receive the maximum benefit from the financial planning experience. James was recognised in 2019 and 2020 in *The Times* as one of the UK's top 100 financial advisers.

James' plan for the future is to help people achieve financial independence for themselves. With his team at Woodfall Wealth, they work with a range of people helping them work out their plans, take action and be held accountable.

Find the Financial Health Check Scorecard at: https://woodfallwealth.scoreapp.com.

🌐 https://woodfallwealth.co.uk

🌐 jameswoodfall.co.uk

🔲 www.linkedin.com/in/james-hadley-woodfall

Lightning Source UK Ltd.
Milton Keynes UK
UKHW020638180221
378924UK00006B/238